hidden faces

of the

Ten Secrets for
Mind/Body Healing from
Kabbalah's
Lost Tree of Life

Sheldon Z. Kramer, Ph.D.
with Mardeene Mitchell

Adams Media Corporation
Holbrook, Massachusetts

Published by
Adams Media Corporation
260 Center Street, Holbrook, MA 02343. U.S.A.
www.adamsmedia.com

ISBN: 1-58062-335-2

Printed in Canada.

J I H G F E D C B A

Library of Congress Cataloging-in-Publication Data
Kramer, Sheldon Z.
Hidden faces of the soul : 10 secrets for mind-body healing from Kabbalah's
lost tree of life / Sheldon Z. Kramer with Mardeene Burr Mitchell.
p.   cm.
Includes bibliographical references.
ISBN 1-58062-335-2
1. Kabala. 2. Self-actualization (Psychology) 3. Mind and body.
I. Mitchell, Mardeene Burr.
BF1611 .K75   2000
135'.47--dc21   99-058267

This publication is designed to provide accurate and authoritative information with regard to
the subject matter covered. It is sold with the understanding that the publisher is not engaged
in rendering legal, accounting, or other professional advice. If legal advice or other expert
assistance is required, the services of a competent professional person should be sought.
— From a *Declaration of Principles* jointly adopted by a Committee of the American Bar
Association and a Committee of Publishers and Associations

This book is available at quantity discounts for bulk purchases.
For information, call 1-800-872-5627.

Happy is the man that findeth wisdom,
And the man that obtaineth understanding.
For the merchandise of it is better
than the merchandise of silver,
And the gain thereof than fine gold.
She is more precious than rubies;
And all the things thou canst desire
are not to be compared unto her.
Length of days is in her right hand;
In her left hand are riches and honour.
Her ways are ways of pleasantness,
And all her paths are peace.
She is a tree of life to them that lay hold upon her,
And happy is every one that holdeth her fast.

—PROVERBS 3:13–18, OLD TESTAMENT, THE BIBLE

Disclaimer From Author and Collaborative Writer/Editor

The author and collaborative writer will have no liability or responsibility to any person(s) or entity with respect to any alleged loss or damage caused directly or indirectly by information contained in this book.

Readers should consult a health care professional if they have questions regarding information or exercises that are included in this book before they engage in using any of them for self-help, especially as it relates to individual concerns regarding mental or physical health.

SHELDON Z. KRAMER, PH.D.
MARDEENE BURR MITCHELL

table of contents

part five
building your face
of stability

part six
balancing your faces

part seven
ultimate unity:
becoming one with
your many faces

acknowledgments

I would like to acknowledge many people who have helped and supported me as I climbed the branches of the Tree of Life. I first acknowledge my many teachers who have helped me rediscover my own roots. A special mention to Rabbi Yitzchak Ginsburg, David Zeller, and Zalman Schacter who have inspired me through their teachings and personal encounters. In addition, I acknowledge my earliest spiritual teachers, including the late Cynthia Pearce and Tom Forman who introduced me, when I was 19 years old, to meditation and the wisdom of the East through the teachings of G. I. Gurjieff, a profound Russian integrator of East–West mystical teachings. I also thank my earliest meditation teachers in Budd Gaya, India, in 1971: Anagrike Munindra, a Buddhist monk, and S. N. Goenka, a wonderful Burmese meditation teacher.

I especially recognize my older brother, Dr. Mark S. Kramer, for his great friendship and support of me, both psychologically and spiritually, throughout my life. I also appreciate and thank my wife, Carmela, and my daughter, Gabriela, who have provided inspiration, as we continue to work on our psychological and spiritual balance.

I am grateful to all the people who were at my side over the years as I developed myself as a teacher of Kabbalah. A small, steady group of folks who were my earliest students deserve recognition:

Maura Richman, Diane and Gordon Kane, Paulette Milander, Murray Milander, Jack and Arlene Scharf, Ted Kagan, Rhonda Mason, Jackie Gang, Elizabeth Fleming, Erica Robbins, Jonathan Smith, Edith and Milton Kodmur, Vince Andragna, Gary Hartman, and Van and Lynn Ballew. My sincere gratitude goes to the many other people who worked with me in the early days of the Tree of Life meditations. I extend a special mention, thanks, and blessings to Gerry Strauss. I thank you all for your support.

I acknowledge my original writing coach, Hal Zina Bennett, who inspired me to write a trade book on the Tree of Life. I appreciate Mardeene Mitchell, for taking an active interest in the Tree of Life teachings and for her dual role as both collaborator and coach. Her emotional support and professional expertise helped me realize the completion of this work. I thank Paula Munier Lee, Senior Editor at Adams Media Corporation, for her enthusiasm and support of this book and for her outstanding practical suggestions for making esoteric material accessible and this book the best it could be.

—SHELDON Z. KRAMER

The Kabbalists' Vision of Creation and the Tree of Life

In the Beginning

The ancient Hidden Ones came together in a place far from the noise and distractions of the city, sequestering themselves deep in the forest. After many years of hard work they had mastered the patience, humility, and meditation skills needed for this sacred encounter. They were ready to learn the story of the universe. They had heard the stories of the others, who, ill prepared to encounter the Creator, had never returned from the abyss. Still, the Ancient Hidden Ones dared to experience the Creator directly. Inspired by the vaulting majesty of their forest cathedral, they closed their eyes, breathed deeply, and embraced the silence.

Suddenly, they were swallowed up by the eternal darkness, where no thing, including themselves, existed—the Lamp of Darkness.

Then began the pulsing, the movement, and the spinning out of control. They plummeted down, down, down, deep into the womb of the earth, spiraling through a maze of roots—the roots of all ancestors.

They somehow knew they need not fear. They looked up and through the unending darkness saw a pinpoint of light. They joyously sped toward it and almost immediately burst into the expanding light, as endless as the darkness behind them.

The Endless Light promptly contracted, creating a vacuum—a pinhole of darkness. In this vast drop of darkness, it directed a sliver of light. Only a sliver, out of love and compassion, for its creation in the physical world would be destroyed by too much brilliant, powerful light! At this moment, nine more contractions took place.

In a flash, the mystics understood the gift and responsibility of creation; they received the vision of the 10 lost vessels. Each of these vessels that held the pulsating light arranged themselves in the shape of a tree—the Tree of Life. The spheres of light were too powerful for the vessels to contain them. The glowing spheres continued to swell and expand and finally exploded into countless sparks. The fireworks of creation illuminated the darkness.

In that moment, the Hidden Ones understood the ancient secrets of the Tree of Life. They also realized that the challenge of all humans is to discover and unify within themselves the 10 faces of enlightenment that illumine every soul!

part one

rediscovering the wisdom of the ages

The 10 Faces of the Soul

1. Unity (*Keter*)
   Feeling at one with yourself, with a Higher Power, with others, and with your inner and outer worlds
2. Wisdom (*Chokmah*)
   An intuitive sense of knowing things
3. Understanding (*Binah*)
   Knowing something only with your analytic mind
4. Love (*Chesed*)
   Genuine caring that leads to kindness and hospitality; the ability to say yes
5. Strength (*Gevurah*)
   Self-restraint and positive Discernment; the ability to say no to yourself and others
6. Compassion (*Tiferet*)
   The blending of Love and Strength
7. Dominion (*Netzach*)
   The ability to take control and to give of yourself; to branch out; to act in the world toward your goals
8. Receptivity (*Hod*)
   The ability to allow yourself to receive and also to monitor your actions
9. Stability (*Yesod*)
   The blending of giving (Dominion) and receiving (Receptivity) to form a stable foundation
10. Faith (*Malchut*)
    The ability to exercise humility and to maintain faith in something greater than yourself, while simultaneously taking responsibility for your thoughts, feelings, and actions toward self and the outside world.

NOTE: The Face of Knowledge is not considered one of the 10 individual faces of the soul, as it is hidden and represents complete enlightenment— the full knowledge of creation with our thoughts, feelings, and actions.

chapter one

Ancient Secrets
for Mind–Body Healing

Their end is embedded in their beginning
and their beginning in their end
like a flame in a burning coal
For the Master is singular
He has no second
And before One, what do you count?
SEFER YETZIRAH (*THE BOOK OF CREATION*)

From the ancient Kabbalists, a Western sect of mystics known as the Hidden Ones, comes an important teaching: "The end is embedded in the beginning."

The whole tree is contained inside the seed. Contained within the protective outer husk of the seed is space. This tiny space reflects the vastness of all existence. The sparks of creation lie in this dark space, ready to catch fire and grow.

Yet, few of us make enough space in our lives to allow these creative sparks to ignite—thereby enabling us to dream, feel, and act according to our own uniqueness. Each of us has the power—to crack open our protective outer masks and release the light to become who we truly are!

The original sparks that exploded from the 10 lost vessels live inside you, ready to light your fire and fuel your new life. The Tree of Life teachings will give you a personal map to guide you in the rediscovery of these truths—your truths.

Picture someone you admire: a favorite professor whose face shines with wisdom and understanding, a best friend whose loving and kind face always comforts you, or a business associate whose confidence radiates from every pore. The faces of other people that you're attracted to parallel your faces that already exist within your soul. How many times have you thought you could never be like someone else? Do what they do? Feel what they feel? Think what they think? You possess all those abilities, just waiting to be cultivated like a seed planted in the ground waiting to sprout.

The Tree of Life teachings reveal that behind the many faces inside, as well as outside, yourself lie the original sparks of creation envisioned by the Kabbalists. The 10 lost vessels on the Tree of Life represent your own 10 faces that make up your personality.

The people to whom we're most drawn have an inner glow about them. They radiate life! Their glow reflects the spark of the Endless Light, which has existed from the beginning of creation and will continue throughout eternity. We want to become like those glowing persons we admire.

When you become the loving gardener of your own seed and tree of life, you will feel more alive. You, too, will radiate life. To do this, you must first take stock of your hidden faces. Which are most prominent? Which need work? Which are in balance; which need balancing?

We often associate the adage, "It's not what you know, but who you know," with material success. To fulfill our complete potential as human beings, we need to know—and express—our many faces. As we allow our hidden faces to glow, we not only realize this full potential, we also attract like-minded people who help us attain our goals and become our best selves.

Balance

Through their vision of the 10 lost vessels, the Hidden Ones recognized that everything humans seek boils down to one thing—a return to balance. Our ultimate joy comes when we learn how to balance all of our 10 faces. It's that simple.

To become "receivers of light," we must balance the self. The more balanced we become, the stronger we become, and the more spiritual light we can receive. The Tree of Life teachings guide us in our journey to become whole, integrated, and happy people (*Tikkun*, self-rectification) as well as to enlighten ourselves with the sparks of creation.

Using the Kabbalah system of self-discovery and enlightenment, you become adept at balancing your 10 faces in the worlds of self, relationships, money, sex, and power.

Gift from the Tree of Life

My own spiritual journey has been an arduous one. For a long time the answers to life's true meaning eluded me. But all along I remained certain of one thing: I intended to find out. Like most young men, I had rebelled against my family's traditions. Put off by my ancestry, in particular, and by organized Western religion, in general, I turned to Eastern philosophies. Mysterious India beckoned, and I traveled to Budd Gaya, where the great Buddha reportedly attained enlightenment and where I, too, hoped to find ecstasy under the Bodhi tree. My Buddhist meditations conjured not inner happiness, as I'd anticipated, but the intense pain of my past. I also realized that the Eastern spiritual path I was pursuing didn't synchronize with my cultural history.

Twenty-five years later, I finally journeyed to Israel, the land of my ancestors. I went with a mixture of anticipation and apprehension, having not yet reconciled my earlier angst about my ancestral heritage. While wandering about the countryside, I happened upon a little town called Sefat, an ancient, timeless village tucked away at the northern end of Galilee, right above Tiberias, where Jesus of Nazareth lived. I instantly felt at home in that place, but did not know why. I also had no idea when I first set foot on the cobblestone roads of Sefat that the experience would change my life forever.

It was wintertime. I walked down the village's narrow, medieval streets, cracked from earthquakes and bombings, and entered the central gallery of the town art colony. There, one particular painting—a six-pointed star that virtually vibrated—fascinated me.

"Who made this picture?" I asked the shopkeeper.

"A Kabbalist," she responded. I knew the Kabbalists were the Nisterim (Hidden Ones), ancient mystics who embraced the Tree of Life teachings and who understood the secrets of creation.

"Does he live in this town?" I queried.

"You don't want to speak with him," she insisted. "Kabbalists are crazy!"

I smiled. "I'm a psychologist. I work with 'crazy' people."

Moments later I stood at the door of the artist's dwelling. A wise old man who looked as though he'd walked out of a mythic story-book opened the door and invited me in. He wore his pitch black hair long, but his most striking feature was his piercing blue eyes, which radiated joy. The artist showed me his artwork, which fasci-nated me, and I asked many questions about the meanings of his work. Our discussions extended over several hours, during which the artist and his art revealed to me the hidden secrets of the mystics.

Awestruck, I felt I had journeyed beyond time. The realization struck me that the knowledge I had sought in other traditions I was discovering within my personal history. By journeying back to my own roots, I unwittingly uncovered the secrets of the roots of Western civilization, right in my own cultural backyard. How many times have we searched far and wide for truth, only to realize we, like Dorothy in the *Wizard of Oz*, always held the key to our own "yellow brick road" home? I returned to America with a sense of exultation. I no longer felt alone.

Shortly after I returned home, I was teaching a seminar on inti-mate relationships. In the middle of the class was an exotic, beau-tiful, yet oddly familiar woman. I asked where was she from.

"A small town in Israel," she replied. "You probably haven't heard of it. Sefat."

I could barely contain my excitement. We were married within the year, exchanging our sacred vows at sunset on a hill in Sefat, overlooking the land of my ancestors. Within another year, my wife was with child. At the age of 42, I wept with joy at the wondrous sight of my beautiful newborn daughter.

The ancient Tree of Life teaches us that the whole is contained in the seed. In my daughter's exotic, almond-shaped eyes that reminded me of large, luminous seeds, I saw everything clearly for the first time. I understood. By returning to the roots of my ancestors and studying diligently the wisdom of the mystics, I had learned how to receive—and she was my gift.

Sowing Seeds of Mystery

Five thousand years ago, only a select few were privy to the secret Tree of Life teachings. So powerful was the wisdom of the Kabbalah, it was passed along from generation to generation orally—to keep it from falling into the wrong hands. Although this ancient Kabbalah and Tree of Life knowledge remains known primarily to only a few mystics and scholars, in recent years a growing number of devotees from various cultures and faiths have embraced the teachings.

The word Kabbalah comes from the Hebrew word *le Kebel*, meaning "to receive." The Kabbalists were the first Jewish mystics, seekers dedicated to receiving the ancient truths that show people how to achieve harmony with themselves, each other, and the natural world.

They believed they could discover the laws of natural relationship by observing the rhythms of nature. The image of the tree evolved out of the Kabbalists' story of creation, probably because the tree poetically embodies the same principles governing human life. Moreover, the tree is a symbol of balance and wholeness embedded deeply in the archetypal roots of the unconscious mind of humanity.

The Tree of Life symbolizes the life force itself. The tree shows us that by rooting ourselves in the earth, we can grow, branching out towards the heavens.

History of Kabbalah's Lost Tree of Life

The Kabbalists originated the mystical interpretation of the creation story found in Genesis. It includes not only philosophical and theological assumptions about the universe, but also scientific wisdom of stars, moon, planets, and other facets of what is now astronomy. Also a treatise on mathematics and physics, these five-thousand-year-old teachings provided insights into what we now know as DNA, the elements, and atomic particles. Scholars consider the first Kabbalist, Abraham, to be the author of Sefer Yetzirah, The Book of Creation, which proposed the then revolutionary theory that everything in this world is connected to everything else.

We are all more universally connected than one might think. Christianity, Judaism, and Islam all come from the same seed—Abraham. The father of Islam, the prophet, Mohammed, is likely one of Abraham's descendants. Some scholars theorize that Abraham also played a significant role in Eastern religions, given the similarity of his name to the East Indian word for high priest, A Brahman.

The Kabbalah, then, consists of the ancient oral teachings that were eventually written down. The Kabbalah texts now surfacing were compiled by scholars who gleaned the teachings from fragments of lost manuscripts. Although the term "Kabbalah" didn't arise until around the twelfth century, clear evidence of Kabbalistic thinking and mystical principles exists from the beginning of Western religions. It is known by different spellings—such as Cabala in Christian circles and as Qabbalah, referring to magical doctrines assumed to come from the Kabbalah.

Kabbalistic mystics delved into the meaning of the stories in the Bible. They found significance in the content of the text as well as in the sequences between stories, the shapes of the letters, and even the order in which the letters appeared. In so doing, they not only gained intellectual insight into the laws of creation, but they also tasted eternity itself by focusing on the sparks of light. They wanted to experience the Creator directly, just as most of us today yearn for a personal relationship with G-d.

NOTE: Throughout this book we will hyphenate "G-d" out of traditional respect for the sacred name.

Blending Ancient with Modern: A Practical Guide for Mind–Body Healing

These teachings gave me a clear, practical map for how to live my life, which I would like to share with you. Because they are very esoteric, the Kabbalah and the Tree of Life teachings are usually difficult to absorb. My aim with this book is to present my understanding of this knowledge and what has been helpful to me in an easier–to–understand format. Using my background as a psychologist, I have blended these ancient teachings into a contemporary psycho–spiritual work that will give you practical ways to heal your body, emotions, and mind, as well as your relationships with others.

However philosophically and theologically challenging the Kabbalistic teachings may seem, these writings nevertheless suggest practical methods of spiritual exploration and discovery that we can apply to our daily lives today.

I've used these methods with great success with clients in my clinical practice. The Tree of Life has provided a simple metaphor that I often use to guide my patients to better health and success—a universal icon that speaks to people of all beliefs and traditions.

The Tree of Life Across Cultures

The mythology and use of the Tree of Life imagery is found across all cultures and world religions. American Indians consider the earth to be their sacred mother. The totem pole is carved from the tree trunk, with masks representing the different animal spirits that guard all of the directions. Spiritual teacher Black Elk said, "It may be that some little root of the sacred tree still lives. Nourish it then, that it may leaf and bloom and fill with singing birds."

In Haitian culture, a pit from a fruit tree may be placed on a newborn child's umbilical cord and planted with the cord in the belly of the earth. As the child grows, so does the tree. The blooming fruit belongs to the child, who can use it to barter or make money. Haitians view the tree as a protection for the child. If the tree grows in an unbalanced way, they believe an evil omen hangs over the child.

(Continued on next page)

(Continued from previous page)

Islamic theology includes many mentions of the Tree of Life. The Holy Book of the Koran states, for example:

> Hast thou not seen how G-d has struck a simultude? A good word is as good as a tree—its roots are firm and its branches are in heaven. It gives its produce every season by the leaves of its Lord. So G-d strikes simultudes for men; happily, they well remember. And the likeness of a corrupt word is as a corrupt tree—uprooted from the earth, having no establishment.
>
> —Qur'an XIV; 27–33

The Sufi mystic Rumi also alludes to the tree as a transcendent symbol of the divine:

> A king, upon hearing of the tree, whose fruit gives immortality, sent an envoy to find it. After many years of fruitless searching, the envoy, in desperation, approached a wise Sheikh, saying; "There is a tree unique in all the corners of the world; its fruit is one of the substance of the Water of Life. I have sought it for years and see no sign except the gibes and ridicule of these merry men." The Sheikh laughed and said to him, "Oh, Simpleton, this is the Tree of Knowledge in the sage—very high and very grand and very farspreading; it is the Water of Life from the all-encompassing Sea of G-d. Thou hast gone after the form, thou hast gone astray; thou canst not find it because thou hast abandoned the reality. Sometimes it is named 'tree,' sometimes 'son;' sometimes it is named 'sea;' sometimes 'clouds.' It is that one thing from which a hundred thousand effects arise; its least effects are everlasting life. Although in essence it is single, it has a thousand effects; innumerable names befit that one thing."

Mark 4:30–36 of the New Testament of the Bible compares the mustard seed with the kingdom of G–d:

> And he said, where unto shall we listen the Kingdom of G–d? Or with what comparison shall we compare it? It is like a grain of mustard seed,

(Continued on next page)

(Continued from previous page)

which, when it is sown in the earth is less than all the seeds that be in the earth; but when it is sown it is grown up, and becometh greater than all herbs, and shooteth out great branches; so that the fowls of the air may lodge under the shadow of it.

The Buddha sat beneath a Bodhi tree and became enlightened. Under the tree, the Buddha focused primarily on the Middle Path, which clearly reflects the concept of balance, but there, he also discovered the Four Noble Truths of life. These new teachings reflected that the more tightly we hold on to things in the extreme, the more we get thrown off balance, because, according to Buddha, all things eventually undergo change and leave us. It is only through achieving equanimity of mind, the middle trunk of the tree, that one can achieve full liberation, peace, and freedom.

The sacred Hindu text of the Upanishads uses the metaphor of the tree and its seeds as the magic of the divine forces:

If someone were to strike once at the root of this large tree, it would bleed, but live. If he were to strike at its stem, it would bleed, but live. If he were to strike at the top, it would bleed but live, pervaded by the living Self. But if the Self were to depart from one of its branches, that branch would wither; if it were to depart from a second, that would wither; if it were to depart from a third, that would wither. If it were to depart from the whole tree, the whole tree would wither.

—Chandogya Upanishad

Note: Some of the above quotes appeared in *Parabola, The Magazine of Myth and Tradition*, fall 1989, which was an excellent issue on the Tree of Life.

The Tree of Life—Healing Symbol

Anxiety and depression are the most common reasons people seek the services of a psychologist. Even those of us who do not seek professional help often suffer from ennui seemingly tied directly to the modern age in which we live. External factors beyond our individual control impinge upon us every day. Many of us struggle to keep our economic, work, family, relationships, and recreational activities in balance. And most of us are exhausted from the demands challenging us on a daily, monthly, and yearly basis. As a result, we accumulate psychological toxins in our minds and bodies, mainly of three kinds: fear, grief, and anger.

Because these negative emotions are so powerful and potentially overwhelming to us, we shut them down and numb ourselves rather than experience the truth of our personal lives. Consequently, many of us face crises in our professional and personal lives or suffer physical illnesses.

Healing requires balancing one's mind *and* body. As my clients tap into their individual emotional difficulties, they become more open and hopeful about new possibilities. By directly experiencing, then expressing, the pain of their lives, they receive a release of abundant energy.

Many times, after some clients release their negative emotions and use their creative imaginations, they feel a physical surge of positive, strong energy emanating from the bottoms of their feet up through the middle spine of their bodies. I then guide them in visualizing their internal experience at that moment. To my amazement, many clients spontaneously envision a tree! And why not? This ancient archetypal icon is a natural map of our bodies. Just like trees, we have roots (feet planted on the ground); a sturdy, centered trunk (spinal cord); lower limbs (legs); middle branches (arms); and upper branches and crown (head), connecting to the sky and heavens above us. The tree also has a right giving side and a left side of strength.

Maria, age 38, consulted with me after divorcing her abusive husband. During her 10–year marriage, she felt totally imprisoned in her own home, unable to be who she really was or to express herself in the relationship. She always had to watch what she said for fear her husband would rebuke her. She believed her husband diminished her spirit. She was a competent and successful business woman, but she'd lost all confidence in herself through wedded hell.

Even after leaving the marriage, Maria held on to tremendous fear, grief, and anger. Overdeveloped on the right side of her tree, she gave too much love. Underdeveloped on the left side of her tree, she was neither discerning enough nor strong enough to speak up for herself.

Using the Tree of Life as her guide, she decided to develop her left branches of Strength. She began to envision herself as a powerful woman who no longer held herself back. She then succeeded in liberating herself by taking charge in her dominion.

In one session, after she was able to express her anger and grief about her marriage, she remembered herself as a dancer in her younger years—how free she felt when she moved, how strong and in control of her body and space! Her whole body transformed in front of me. Her rigid muscular face relaxed, transforming her frozen expression into a radiant smile. Her body loosened as her breathing expanded.

As she continued to stand and focus on her breathing, I asked her to come up with an image for that moment. She stated, "I am in the middle of a grove surrounded by clear blue sky. I am a tree." I asked her to describe what she felt like as a tree. Through tears she spoke with increasing conviction, "I am beautiful; I am strong. I have roots that ground me, and I'm connected to the heavens. I am powerful, and I can do and be what I want."

I asked her to repeat the words, "I am strong and powerful," qualities she had lost in her marriage. When she repeated these words, she felt an inner sturdiness in the middle of her body that she had not experienced in a long time. She experienced a growing sense of faith and reverence for her roots, which had connected her to the earth and always protected her.

In that moment, Maria achieved balance—a unity of thinking, feeling, and action. She was rewarded by a tremendous sense of joy and Unity (upper crown of the tree). She stood up straighter, prouder—and thanked me for the gift she had received.

I said to her, "The gift did not come from me. It came from the universe and the Creator, who remind us of our wholeness and beauty when we forget."

Like Maria, you can use the Tree of Life as a map to guide you to a new life. In this book, we'll explore the principles of the Tree of Life and learn how to apply the techniques to transform your daily life. We'll light the way with examples of the teachings in action in the lives of three of my clients, Michael, Cynthia, and Jeff.

Along with Michael, Cynthia, and Jeff, you'll fill out your own Tree of Life map, assessing where you are in your evolution, and facilitating your journey to health, prosperity, and spiritual awareness.

Benefits of Mastery of the Tree of Life

Learning the ancient secrets of the Kabbalah allows us to live:

- ∾ In freedom from worry
- ∾ In harmony with the laws of nature
- ∾ In receptivity to G-d's Gifts
- ∾ In knowing our limits
- ∾ In balance with receiving and giving
- ∾ In appreciation that less can be more
- ∾ In prosperity with money—money does grow on trees!
- ∾ In truth with our visions
- ∾ In love with personal Intimacy
- ∾ In action, reaping the fruits of professional success

THE TREE OF LIFE

SPIRIT

UNITY
Keter

MIND

UNDERSTANDING	KNOWLEDGE	WISDOM
Binah	*Daat*	*Chokmah*

EMOTION

STRENGTH	COMPASSION	LOVE
Gevurah	*Tiferet*	*Chesed*

ACTION

RECEPTIVITY	STABILITY	DOMINION
Hod	*Yesod*	*Netzach*

FAITH
Malchut

Humility	*Roots of Reverence*	*Responsibility*

chapter two

Overview of the Tree of Life

In their vision of creation, the Hidden Ones saw 10 vessels of light in the shape of a tree—reflecting the 10 faces of the soul within each human being. The Tree of Life symbolizes the body as a whole as well as the unseen dynamic energies behind each face. The tree trunk unites and nourishes the rest of the tree through its biochemical processes, just as our central nervous system connects our brain and spinal cord to the rest of our bodies. The left and right branches of the Tree of Life represent the left and right sides of our brains as well as of our bodies.

The Power of Three

The Kabbalists addressed in a simple but profound way the three forces of expanding, contracting, and balancing energy states. This triad of balanced power forms the core of natural law. These three forces can be seen in the atom—and, indeed, in our DNA—as the expansive proton, the contracting electron, and the balancing neutron.

The esoteric literature of major world religions also describe these three forces: as *Chokmah* (wisdom), *Binah* (understanding), and *Daat* (knowledge) in Judaism; as the Father, Son, and Holy Ghost in Christianity; as Brahma (the creator), Vishnu (the sustainer), and Shiva (the destroyer) in Hinduism; as Allah (the balancing force),

Mohammed (the active energy), and Imam (the 12 receivers and dispensers of knowledge) in Islam.

A child is the miraculous third force derived from the union of two parents, forming the sacred trinity that perpetuates the human species.

Finally, yes, the tree—like a pyramid or triangle—has its three main parts—the roots, the trunk, and the branches. Later in this book you will discover that the Tree of Life is further expanded or divided into sacred triads. However, we will begin by visualizing the tree and its roots, trunk, and branches, using the diagram of the Tree of Life on page 27. (The figure's back is facing the reader.)

The Roots

The tree's roots denote where the rubber meets the road— where we walk on Earth. It also signifies where we can submerge and reconnect with our roots, with the knowledge of our ancestors. This reverence for our roots assures us that the earth holds the seeds of creation, which are always at our disposal. When we feel scared, insecure, lost, or thrown off balance, our basic roots hold us close to the ground. We know we are not alone.

The Trunk

Rising up between and connecting the roots and branches is the trunk, the tree's base, or spine. The trunk manifests the powerful fulcrum that balances the basic building blocks of the universe, while holding and distributing the branches. It is the apex of the powerful law of three. This middle trunk serves as the balancing point of all that exists—between the right and left sides of the tree as well as between the yes and no, heart and mind, body and soul, humility and power, child and adult of every human. Representing enduring stability, the trunk contains the ancestral rings that tell us when to follow our instincts and when to approach a situation analytically. Our trunks provide us with the commonsense ability to flow with the forces of nature, rather than fighting upstream against them. It is the stable place where we feel balanced and at peace, content, knowledgeable, and compassionate.

The Branches

Sometimes branches bend and stretch, reaching out hungrily in different directions, expanding, stretching up and out, searching for more. Sometimes they whisper a gentle warning to stop the growth and listen, to lie dormant and rest. In stormy weather, they stoop to the ground under the weight of opposing forces and send a graphic warning when they are about to break. In the warmth of the sun or on soft breezy evenings, they rustle quietly, peacefully, content to settle into a calm, inner place.

Ancient Faces

The Biblical stories of Abraham's descendants illustrate in a fascinating way the balancing of the natural forces on a human level. They speak of certain leaders—men and their women partners—who became the archetypal faces representing the different qualities on the Tree of Life. Interestingly, the Biblical stories portray these ancient heroes and heroines in all their humanness, with their many human frailties. These ancient archetypes—along with our contemporary heroes and heroines—demonstrate these energies, both heroic and human, in action in their worlds. Even heroes must work on their shortcomings!

Reconnecting the 10 Faces of Your Soul: Balancing Your Inner Sacred Triads

Now that you have an overall picture of the concepts and teachings, you're ready to take a closer look at the Tree of Life and the individual qualities or hidden energies comprising each face.

This section of the book gives you a quick, yet, more in depth overview of how the faces of the Tree of Life are organized and interact with each other.

The Unifying Realm

The highest face is the crown, above the head, at the top of the tree where one connects to the heavens—denoting Unity.

Contained in the face of unity are all the other faces on the Tree of Life. All the ten faces can be experienced as one face! In addition, each face below the face of unity also contains all the other ten faces. For example, under the thinking realm, there is the face of wisdom. Contained in the face of wisdom are the other qualities of the Tree of Life blended with wisdom, i.e. unity in wisdom, wisdom in wisdom, understanding in wisdom, love in wisdom, strength in wisdom, compassion in wisdom, dominion in wisdom, receptivity in wisdom, stability in wisdom, faith in wisdom. The same unifications can occur in the face of understanding, i.e. unity in understanding, wisdom in understanding, understanding in understanding, love in understanding, etc.

Each of the faces contains all the other faces, and all the faces integrate into one face. These faces reflect Mind, Emotion, and Action.

The Thinking Realm (Mind)

Balanced thought is Knowledge (*Daat*), a hidden face that reveals itself only when the other 10 faces are balanced. However, one can visualize this ideal Knowledge between the faces of Unity and Compassion. The expanded manifestation of Knowledge on the right indicates the quality of Intuition or Wisdom (*Chokmah*). The contracted energetic face of Knowledge on the left depicts the face of Understanding (*Binah*), the ability to analyze.

The Feeling Realm (Emotion)

In the realm of Emotion, the natural balance is called Mercy or Compassion (*Tiferet*). The expansive manifestation (right side) of Compassion is Love and Kindness (*Chesed*). The contracted manifestation of feeling (left side) reflects Strength through Discernment, or exercising good judgment (*Gevurah*).

The Doing Realm (Action)

In the Action realm, the balanced energetic face is Stability (*Yesod*). This comprises the firm foundation constructed in the fulcrum (middle trunk) of the tree. The face of Dominion (*Netzach*) expands itself into the world from the right side. The face of Receptivity (*Hod*) contracts on the left.

The Grounding Realm

The last balanced face reflects total groundedness and meticulous responsibility—the ability to respond with Action (*Malchut*). This responsibility derives from the attitude of faith, humility, and a reverence for our roots, recognizing that everything tied to our roots was created before we existed.

Introduction to Assessing and Cultivating Your Growth

Balancing yourself spiritually and psychologically involves understanding the interplay between these 10 dynamic faces. You must also pay attention to those things you need to work on inside yourself with relation to these hidden energies behind your faces. Keep in mind that this growth follows a circular, rather than a linear, pattern of progression. All the faces of your soul are interconnected with your branches and with the steps you live. And growth is always ongoing.

Yet, a book is linear by definition. To help you achieve balance, this book orders the faces in the way I've found most helpful to my clients. However, you may decide you need to jump ahead to the face that needs immediate assistance, the one that's really hiding and blocking your progress. Whether you read this book straight through or skip around as you deem necessary, the goals remain the same: to achieve stability and balance of yourself at will; to uncover and use all these energies successfully; and to radiate light in your inner and outer worlds from all your faces.

Exercise 1: Assessing Your Personality Style

Would you classify yourself as a predominantly thinking, feeling, or action-oriented person? If you are more intellectually identified, you may need to learn how to open up your feelings. If you are more connected to your feelings, you may need to learn how to think more methodically. If you are a "doer" who is more action-oriented, you may need to learn to explore your thoughts and feelings before you act.

Write a paragraph about the realm of experiencing (thinking, feeling, or doing) you believe is your dominant style in daily life. Write a second paragraph about your weakest style.

The Juggling Act in the Real World

The Tree of Life map guides us through life by navigating us along the pathways of the 10 sacred qualities, or faces, we must integrate to reach our destination—our soul's completion. The map shows us how to balance and release our light energies, which were hidden until now. (Look at the illustration at the end of this chapter.)

I have found that the best way to teach the process of unifying all your faces of energy is to encourage you to see yourself as a juggler, learning to juggle these balls of light, in different combinations, and eventually keeping them all up in the air at the same time.

Ultimate psychological and spiritual responsibility comes from keeping these balls balanced and the tree aligned, and from knowing how to use your will to do these things consciously. When you have achieved that, you will have mastered your tree of life.

Picture the Tree of Life and each of the faces as a ball of light. Now, imagine you are the juggler, keeping all the balls moving in a circular motion in the air at the same time. That's quite a juggling act!

Moment to moment, you feel emotions, stop to think, then act, care, and then say no. You try to bring all the laws together and glimpse the vision of Unity, experiencing a moment of ecstasy. In awe, you realize you can juggle 10 balls, 10 laws of nature, all at once, while walking on a tightrope! And you're only a human being. Others, too, stand in awe of the juggler, who, like a circus performer, can do something many of us cannot.

Wow! Now, you've envisioned your ability to juggle the 10 faces of your soul, the balls of light gracefully circling around you. You've seen it in your mind's eye, felt it in your heart, and believe in it. But can the juggler do it in real life? That's the test.

In your day-to-day life, the faces of your soul, just like the circus juggler's balls, will rotate or change differently at different times. In reality, you sometimes have to make one ball more dominant than the others. Some will rotate in the background, while others will go straight up and down.

Juggle the ball of Love with the ball of Strength, then add the middle ball of Compassion (the level of Emotion) to keep you moving. Add another three balls from the Action level: giving out to the world, receiving, and the middle ball that stabilizes your action. Got 'em going? These six balls (energies) represent the six directions of the world—North, South, East, West, up and down. Once you get these six balls going, you can then achieve balance—the center of all directions. Does this sound familiar to those acquainted with American Indian wisdom? All truths are universal.

Try keeping these balls juggling at the same time in the air—surely the feat of a magician. Uh-oh. Sometimes when you're trying to keep love going while also trying to be discerning, you drop the love ball! So you're juggling these six balls. Uh-oh. You let the expansion ball dominate, now you've spent too much money, dropped the left ball of analyzing and discerning, and ended up bankrupt. Life clearly challenges us.

This is not an easy journey. It takes discipline. But you can learn to love the process while you become the expert juggler of your life. You can switch between inspiration and grounding.

Learn the art of Discernment—ask yourself, am I saying what I really mean and doing what I really want? You can move back and forth between expansion and contraction, finding the middle ground, the trunk. In so doing, you will activate and revel in your endurance, emotional strength (left), and intuitive beliefs (right). You'll feel compassion for the process as well as the pain and ecstasy of it. You'll experience empathy for the people involved (center), leading to giving (right) and the need to act on the lower branch (right). Then you'll monitor your actions (left), ever mindful of how you feel, think, and behave—always remembering your basic roots, acknowledging the good in it, and sharing your knowledge.

Secrets of the Seven Days of the Week

The bottom seven of the 10 faces on the Tree of Life correspond with the seven days of the week.

The first six represent the active energies in everyday life, beginning with Sunday, which is Love, a day when we're more open. Monday is Strength, which enables us to discriminate what we need to do at the beginning of the work week. Tuesday, Compassion, a blending of the first two faces, motivates us to stay in balance with our actions on Wednesday, the day of Dominion, when we take control toward realizing goals we set to accomplish that week. Thursday, Receptivity, allows us to monitor what we are doing, giving us Stability on Friday, when we reap the benefits of our active labor.

On the seventh day, G-d stopped for a day of rest. So, too, do we rest and honor the point of creation, which contains everything, because it is the balancing point. The seventh force is a receptacle holding all the other energies on Earth—like woman receives the seed from man and holds it in her womb, nurturing it. The seventh day, the Sabbath (*Shabbat*), is Faith through responsibility, which honors the feminine.

Coincidentally, this book took its own form and mysteriously ended up with seven sections.

Tree of Life Meditations:
Pathways to Master Your Many Faces

Throughout this book you will find techniques designed to cultivate the specific attributes found in the different branches of the Tree of Life. The main technique taught by the Kabbalists is meditation. They believed and taught that what you think creates your reality. Inspired thinking (often experienced in meditation) lights up your heart and produces inspired action.

These meditations actually work as behavioral modifications. You visualize the result you want, absorbing it into your body so you can manifest that result in the physical world.

Most of the breakthroughs my clients have experienced have come through these imaging/meditation techniques. Many of the most helpful, colorful, and graphic images emerged in sessions and meditations. One woman, who wanted to learn how to say no to things she didn't want to do, saw herself brandishing a flashing sword and riding a white steed into the camps of the enemy. This powerful image helped her learn to see herself as a strong woman capable of saying no and meaning it—and soon she found herself actually saying no and meaning it. She became the image of Strength she had imagined in her meditations.

Similarly, one of my male clients was so used to being in command and giving the orders, that he was insensitive to others and unable to accept advice, hugs, or compliments from others. He wanted to learn how to be more open to others—and thus pictured himself as a huge gilded cup, a symbol of Receptivity.

Many clients return to the image of the tree when they want to feel comfort, stability, and groundedness. When they want to feel inspired, they envision themselves climbing into the uppermost branches of the tree.

Contemporary Profiles

Many of my clients have been extremely pleased with the tangible results they have gained in their lives thanks to Tree of Life practices and meditations. Some amazing transformations took place when people utilized the teachings and techniques that I share with you in this book.

You will read several vignettes of real men, women, and young people who were able to resolve myriad issues they had been struggling with using the Tree of Life concepts and process. Of course identities and some details have been changed to protect privacy; in some cases, the people are composites. But in all cases, the lessons learned are accurate, and the changes that took place are true. You will get to know three particular contemporaries and their stories in greater depth.

Michael

When I first met Michael, he was a quiet and earnest but unhappy ex-military officer who didn't know how to break out from the confines of his military upbringing and training. He was paralyzed in his job-hunting efforts after retirement, emotionally estranged from his family, and seriously depressed. This book shares how Michael, through his willingness to work and change, opened himself up, became kinder and more confident, rediscovered his childhood soul, and rekindled his buried dreams. Ultimately, he created happiness in his true vocational calling.

Cynthia

Cynthia is an attractive, intelligent, and formerly self-effacing educator who, in spite of her intellect, gave away too much of herself, especially to men. You will learn how Cynthia, through her Tree of Life work, learned clarity and how to balance Love with Strength. She became more direct about what she wanted and needed, no longer acquiescing to others at her expense. She blossomed in both career and relationships.

Jeff

Jeff is an outgoing, dynamic, and highly successful entrepreneur whose many ventures allowed him no time for his personal life. He also became extremely over-anxious when situations careened out of control—which happened on a regular basis. This book shares how the Tree of Life taught Jeff monitoring skills that have had a tremendous impact on his peace of mind, his health and family, and on his expanding business success.

The Tree of Life

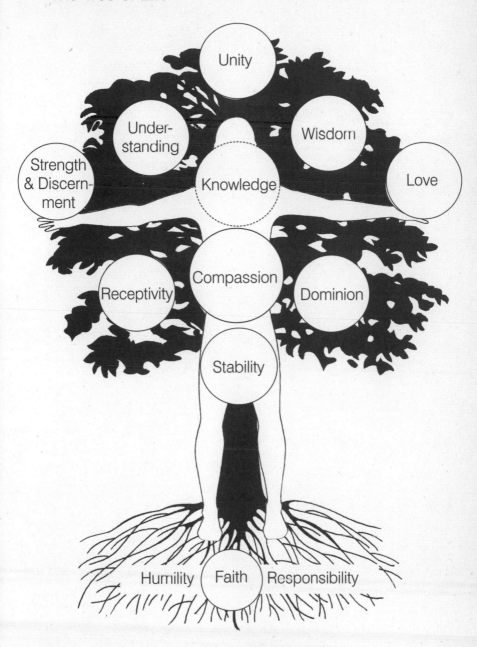

Roots of Reverence

part two

returning to
your roots

Picture yourself strolling in a lush garden or rain forest. Nature's new beginnings—sprouting green vegetation and blossoming flowers—surround you. You come across a stately tree, ancient, symmetrical, balanced, and you realize it has existed for many generations before you. Moved by this tree, you sit on the soft and comforting soil beneath the grand tree. You slowly survey the landscape and breathe in deeply. A sense of awe at the perfection of this magical place fills you. As you embrace the feeling of reverence for the roots beneath you, you grow calm and peaceful inside. You derive comfort in the knowledge that the earth has supported you since your birth and will continue to nourish you until your death.

You look up through the branches of this tree of life, past the crown to the sunlight beaming through the branches, and a delightful tingle spreads through your body. You realize you are not alone. As you experience the grandeur of humility, you accept you do not control everything. Then a wave of love—indeed, relief— sweeps over you.

To heal and rebalance ourselves—and to pursue our dreams— we must have faith the Creator will always take care of us, no matter what, as we move through life. Only then do we feel safe to take the steps needed to climb up and down the trunk of our lives. Only then can we learn how to branch out in multiple directions congruent with our individual selves.

chapter three

The Face of Faith—*Malchut*

Faith contains the power of growth. A person with perfect faith will grow and develop . . . regardless of the obstacles or difficulties he may encounter, nothing will throw him off-course. He will accept whatever he experiences with patience.

—NACHMAN OF BRESLOV, *ADVICE ON TRUTH AND FAITH*

Getting ahead in a different profession requires avid faith in yourself. You must be able to sustain yourself against staggering blows. There is no code of conduct to help beginners. That is why some people with mediocre talent, but with great inner drive, go further than people with vast superior talent.

—SOPHIA LOREN, ACTRESS

Ever since the creation of the world his invisible nature has been clearly perceived in the things that have been made.

—ROMANS 1:20, NEW TESTAMENT, THE BIBLE

In the marvelous children's book *The Carrot Seed*, Ruth Krauss depicts the beauty of a child's spirit that trusts his environment with pure innocence and optimism. In this story, the child plants a carrot seed in a sunny spot in his garden. His parents and siblings discourage him, telling him no kid can grow a carrot tree. Undaunted, the child tends his garden, steadfastly pulling weeds and watering. Day after day he comes out to the garden to see whether his efforts have paid off, and day after day he endures his naysayers "I told you so's." At last, one sweet day, a carrot sprout awaits him. The last scene shows him carrying off a gigantic, beautiful carrot in his little wagon, to the amazement of those who doubted.

As adults, we somehow lose that inner, childlike spirit of innocence, optimism, and trust in the world. Many of us, including some of my clients, have lost their faith. Overwhelmed with doubt and insecurity, they seek consultation.

Recently two of my clients came in for help in dealing with serious personal losses: Anne, a mother who had lost her nine-year-old daughter in a car accident, and Evelyn, a physician with lung cancer.

I found myself questioning my efforts to help these women build their self-confidence. I wondered how I could restore their faith? When the natural rhythms of life bring inevitable losses, we feel we have nothing secure to hang on to. This often happens in middle-age, when our illnesses or disappointments demonstrate our limitations, our children mature and leave home, and our parents age and die.

During such mid-life "crises," many people undertake spiritual quests. However, others, perhaps disillusioned in their youths by concepts of G-d they could not embrace, struggle on in frustration. For example, some drug- and alcohol-addicted people find it difficult to participate in twelve-step programs, because they can't accept the notion of a Higher Power. However, it is important for some people to find alternative approaches to conceptualizing and practicing their spirituality. The search for alternative perspectives in understanding life's inevitable challenges and sufferings is important for both psychological and spiritual balance.

The Tree of Life—A Natural Metaphor

The Tree of Life teachings offer a breath of fresh air to people who lack a spiritual inclination or hope for the future. Yet, nature provides a brilliant metaphor, if not proof, that something miraculous, something beyond mere physical recognition, occurs moment to moment in our world. The laws of nature are very predictable; we can *depend* absolutely on the occurrence and existence of certain things every day. The sun rises and sets. Seasons change. The Earth continuously revolves, assuring the gravity that keeps us upright and grounded wherever we walk.

Accordingly, when we trust the forces of nature to help us grow—whether physically, emotionally, mentally, or spiritually—we acknowledge the creative spark within, which perpetuates what we need to manifest. Realizing we are co-creators in our lives, we learn to appreciate these eternal forces, which develops a deepening sense of humility. We then understand that we achieved whatever our accomplishments not alone but through the spiritual powers within us.

Ancient Roots

The Kabbalah refers to the Tree of Life's roots, or the ground on which the tree stands, as *Malchut*, Hebrew for "kingship," or "foundation." When the things in the world are in balance, we feel in greater control of our lives, like kings leading their kingdoms. We also learn to depend on others for help in achieving our goals. Think of a waterbed in the depths of the ocean. This bed of water, a common Kabbalistic image, is a force that contains the waters of life. A feminine energy similar to a woman's womb, which holds the seeds of human creation inside the body, the waterbed also serves as the receptacle for the seeds of Earth's vegetation. This energy forms the basis of everything, the foundation of all existence.

When we acknowledge Earth's bountiful gifts, we can rely on the earth for sustenance, as a trusting child with stable parents can go to them to ask for support free of fear and open-hearted. When we acknowledge our prayers and wishes to ourselves and others, we

come to embrace the world as a place that graciously provides what
we need.

Biblical Archetype of Faith:
King David—Symbol of *Malchut*

The Old Testament figure of King David embodies the quality
of *Malchut*. The impeccable warrior who unifies his kingdom,
David demonstrates extreme power in his kingly actions, while
simultaneously pursuing his heavenly inspirations—singing,
writing poetry, and playing the harp. The songs of David, Psalms,
are still known and beloved today.

The ability to act courageously in the world while embracing
humility and faith is the hallmark of *Malchut*. Obviously, that is
the ideal. Yet, the Bible depicts David, like all Biblical heroes,
with human foibles and weaknesses as well as strengths. His
tremendous energy and strong vision enabled him to achieve
kingly status and to unify his warring kingdom. Some might
think of David's motivating force as an agenda—at times, his
own. A master politician, he knew how to manipulate others to
get things done. He succeeded in overcoming King Saul and that
dynasty. When he became king, he horrified his supporters by
coveting Bathsheba and sending her husband to his sure death in
battle so he could have her.

Notwithstanding, David got the job done. He fought superbly
against many warring factions and unified the nation. A warrior of
tremendous heart, David cared about his people and asked the
Creator not to punish them too harshly. His music and poetry gave
him a direct line to the Creator of all life, which facilitated his
vision and success. Sent by G–d to restore the kingdom, David ful-
filled his job with impunity. David mastered all his faces: grounded
in reverence for his roots and faith and inspired to act with compassion and heroism!

Exercise 2: How Deep Is Your Faith?

Review this brief list of qualities to determine how trust and faith are operating in your life at this moment. Consider how closely each trait applies to your current state of being, putting a check next to those items that are more true than false about you.

1. I begin each day optimistic about the future.
2. I accept myself and others.
3. I trust my environment.
4. I rely on others, confident I'll get my needs easily met.
5. I flow with change, accepting it as inevitable.
6. I believe in a power greater than myself.
7. I am self-assured.
8. I feel grateful.
9. I graciously surrender to my Higher Power.
10. I accept responsibility to do what is "right" now and for future generations.

Cultivating Your Trust / Renewing Your Faith

Once we acknowledge the power of the earth to provide what we need for our health and our lives, most of us can cultivate a sense of a Higher Power within ourselves. Developing this sense subsequently increases our sense of well-being and gratitude. In fact, one way to cultivate greater faith is to begin every day by consciously acknowledging the little things we are grateful for in our daily lives.

In today's highly interconnected world, most of us can pick up a telephone or dash off a fax or e-mail, and in the blink of an eye reach someone who can potentially meet our needs. When we are sick, for instance, we usually can get help within a short period of time. Synchronicity moments occur frequently: We think about friends, and they call us; or we consider doing something new, and articles on that topic pop out at us or people offer helpful information out of the blue.

We can all embrace this invisible network of interconnectedness. When we honor this sense of oneness, we develop the tenacity and patience to tend the gardens of our lives, like the child in the book tended his carrot seed. That little boy knew to wait for a root system to develop—clearly demonstrating an innate inner wisdom. How many dreams do we give up on when we don't get immediate results?

As we develop greater faith and deep respect for our roots, we accept our greater responsibility to the Higher Power to help the world become a more loving and secure place. This signals the birth of our true conscience and budding spirituality.

Faith Conquers Tragic Loss

When her nine–year–old daughter died, Anne could barely go on living. To help restore her balance and reassure her faith that death was not meaningless, with my guidance she envisioned and spoke with the spirit of her dead child. She wept when she heard her child's wise counsel, telling her she (Anne) had been closed off for a long time, even before the accident. It was time to trust other people and to let them in, enabling her to grow from the experience.

As Anne became more open and trusting, she did grow and her circle of friends grew, helping to fill the emptiness left by her child's parting.

Releasing Control

A physician in her fifties, Evelyn was used to being totally in control. She came to me shaken by the prognosis that her lung cancer was terminal and feeling vulnerable like her patients. She had to deal with her illness and mortality, without knowing all the answers and unsure of the outcome.

Together, we worked on renewing her faith and hope. During meditations, she focused on learning to trust her innate wisdom in her body—telling her when to rest, when to work. She expanded her ability to love herself and others. She increased her Strength by setting boundaries, telling the partners in her practice when she needed to work less. She embraced the mystery of life and experienced the peace that comes with trusting and with letting go of the need to control. She was able to face her illness with a new sense of serenity and empowerment.

Extremely anxious about work, Jeff never took time off. He rarely scheduled time for himself, and he paid little attention to what was really going on in his life. As his coach, I literally tore him away from his job and took him on retreats.

He learned that to clear his mind, he first needed to relax and spend time alone or with me on self-reflection and getting centered. He discovered this well-spent time of renewal restored his faith in himself and enabled him to direct his life in more meaningful ways. By letting go of control and by learning to lean on others, he developed more trust and faith.

Developing Fertile Ground

To develop rich soil in which to grow, you must learn to become seed-like in consciousness. Many of us are easily distracted by our internal thoughts and feelings as well as by our external environments. Yogis in India say we humans possess a "monkey mind" that moves repeatedly from one branch to another. We need to develop the ability to still our minds and emotions. First, you must understand the nature of the seed.

A seed is a very precious commodity. However, when you look at a seed, you see nothing more than a wooden husk.

If you break open a seed you find space. Similarly, when you develop the ability to meditate and focus, you also discover inner spaciousness. From this seed-like concentration you then can begin to expand into your world.

Faith and Biological Time Clocks

Approaching her fortieth birthday, Martha despaired over finding a suitable partner with whom to have a family. She often felt depressed and full of self-doubt. Even her heartbeat served as a reminder that her biological clock was ticking, ticking, ticking.

I encouraged her to be open, to visualize the man of her dreams, and to communicate her need for a good partner to as many people as possible. Despite her embarrassment, she did so.

One day I got an emergency call from her. She was crying and ready to give up. "I need to start the procedure for a test tube baby," she wailed. I reminded her that many women over 40 give birth to children and encouraged her to think of test tube conception only as a last resort. Shortly after, she called to tell me she had met a terrific guy who was a little older than she and had been married previously, but had no children. They hit it off. Within the year, they got married, she got pregnant, and she gave birth to a healthy baby girl. Years later, she still talks about her great match with her husband.

What was the secret of Martha's success? According to the Tree of Life, revering your roots and faith humbles you and enables you to put aside your pride so you can put out your needs to the universe. Marsha did that, and when she least expected it, one of her clients fixed her up with a friend—and bingo, a match made in heaven!

Exercise 3: Meditation for Renewing Faith

1. Sit in a comfortable position on the floor or a hard–backed chair. Keep your spine erect.
2. Slowly inhale and exhale through your nose, focusing your full attention on your breathing. After a minute or two, inhale quickly and deeply through your nose, hold the breath for a few seconds, then let it out slowly through your mouth. Repeat two more times .
3. Now, breathe normally, focusing on your inhaling and exhaling. Experience the air moving in and out of your nose. Tune into those sensations as you feel the air gently moving in and out of your body.
4. Take another deep breath quickly through your nose. Hold it, then let it out slowly through your mouth. Repeat two more times.
5. Return to breathing naturally in and out of your nostrils. Feel yourself calm down and focus more intensely, growing increasingly more relaxed.
6. Envision yourself sitting on the earth's floor surrounded by beautiful trees—their roots securely burrowed in the ground beneath you and their upper branches forming a canopy above you. Experience yourself as part of the earth, of nature, acknowledging you are an integral but not the only part of the larger surrounding.
7. One by one, identify the things you have tried to control and release them. As they float away and out of your realm, take refuge in the knowledge that something greater than yourself has carried you this far in your life. Then let the qualities of humility and faith in the Greater Power, surrounding all on Earth, enter and fill you.
8. Recognize that a Greater Power protects you and that you possess the ability to help the Creator perform positive work in the world. Embrace the creative energies already at your disposal, using them to make your life more meaningful, purposeful, and stable.

Meditation on the Tetragrammaton: Sacred Letters of Faith

The Tetragrammaton (Yud-Hey-Vav-Hey), written horizontally from right to left

The Bible's book of Psalms says to keep the name of G-d before you always. Accordingly, the ancient Kabbalists visualized these four Hebrew letters (representing G-d) to keep their faith alive.

The Tetragrammaton (Yud-Hey-Vav-Hey), written vertically from top to bottom.

When written vertically from top to bottom, the Tetragrammaton representing the Creator (G-d) depicts the shape of a person and/or a tree.

Secrets of the Sacred Letters

In Christian circles, these four letters represent Jehovah or *Yahweh*. The true pronunciation of the highest emanation of the name, G-d, is unknown and considered lost. The Old Testament says that Moses at the burning bush heard the name *Eheyeh Asher Eheyeh* (I am that I am).

When the letters are written vertically, these letters can depict the Tree of Life. They can also resemble a drawing of a human figure.

Together these four letters provide a code, or symbolic mandala, for our Higher Self, representing the whole Tree of Life. The Yud at the very top (vertical), or far right (horizontal), looks like a seed or sperm, representing the male aspect of humanity. The first Hey, seen as a womb, is the female principle. The Yud and upper Hey both relate to the spiritual facets of our souls. The phallic shape of Vav also symbolizes male energy, like its upper counterpart, Yud. The bottom Hey again represents the female component of humanity. The Vav and lower Hey both correspond to the physical manifestations of our soul. Thus, the four letters in combination integrate the spiritual and material worlds and represent the union of opposing male and female energies.

Each of the letters of the Y-H-V-H correlate to a specific number. (All twenty-two letters of the Hebrew alphabet relate to numbers. For example, in the English alphabet, the letter A would equal one; B would equal two, etc.) Yud is the tenth letter of the alphabet; Hey is the fifth; and Vav is the sixth. The sum of the numbers associated with these four letters (10+5+6+5) is 26. If you then add together the two and six contained within 26, it equals eight. The number eight turned on its side becomes the infinity symbol.

How Michael Regenerated His Faith

My client Michael's experience reconnecting with faith may inspire you. Although conflicted and depressed, he was willing to learn and eventually achieved a gratifying victory.

With me, Michael was a very friendly, pleasant man. However, with others he apparently was extremely quiet and closed off. People judged him to be arrogant and aloof, which hurt him in his relationships. Michael hid all his insecurities behind his military bearing. After retiring from a lifelong career in the military, he had grown increasingly more anxious and depressed. Job-hunting was an excruciating process for him that was not producing results. Accustomed to a structured work environment, he was reluctant to take risks. His body language and manner communicated he neither wanted nor needed help from anybody. Wishing not to appear "weak," he refused to show vulnerability. Like Evelyn, the physician, he was used to calling the shots. The pain that produces a compulsive need to control comes from our ancestral roots, our inner family history, which we will explore in chapter 13, "Drawing Wisdom from Your Ancestral Rings." People who resist leaning on others also resist leaning on a higher force.

During one of our conversations about root qualities, he revealed he admired people who had faith. However, he stayed away from church, because he couldn't admit weakness or make himself vulnerable in front of the Creator. I suggested he needed to reconcile himself perhaps by talking with Christ about his arrogance. This was very threatening to him. Nevertheless, he agreed, and I went with him to his church in a very unusual intervention.

We were alone in the church that morning, and were surprised to learn it was Ash Wednesday! Ash Wednesday occurs at the beginning of Lent (a time of letting go of misdeeds before Easter). It embraces the quality of humility, reminding ourselves of the "ashes to ashes" passage from the Bible. For us to show up by chance in church on that particular day was serendipitous at the very least.

I smeared the mark of ashes on his forehead, and he did the same on mine. We meditated. Then Michael called out to G-d to ask for help, humbling himself and crying. It was a major breakthrough, which began with a leap of faith and propelled his transformation. From that point on, he took more risks and opened himself to other people, no longer too proud to ask questions about work.

part three

reaching for
knowledge (mind)

Mind

Understanding and cultivating your whole tree begins with mastering the upper triad of the Mind. Imagination coupled with the ability to think clearly will help you to develop yourself utilizing the Tree of Life teachings.

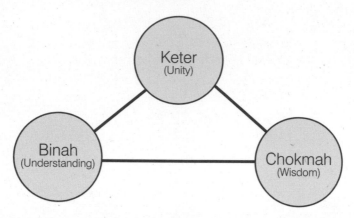

Branches of Knowledge

Study the diagram depicting the upper branches of the Tree of Life, called the branches of Knowledge. This Triad of the Mind works to clarify the direction in which you want to move. The right side contains the face of Wisdom (*Chokmah*) and the left the face of Understanding (*Binah*); the top of the tree is called Unity (*Keter*, which means "crown"). Comparing the other triadic diagrams (Emotion and Action), which appear in later chapters, reveals the upper Mind branches form an upward triangle, whereas the middle and lower branches form upside–down triangles.

The Tree of Life acknowledges our need to become whole by also grounding ourselves in emotions and actions (upside down triangles), while also accepting inspiration from the heavens (upper triangle), which connect to the unifying center (*Keter*). Combining the upside down triangle with the regular shaped triangle forms the geometric shape of the six-pointed star.

The Tree of Life teachings assert that when you reach toward the upper triad of Knowledge, you can experience a vast expansiveness of mind. This inner spaciousness connects to the seat of your creativity. When inspired, like a magician you create "some thing" from "no thing." However, before you can bring this something into existence—whether it be a more balanced life or a specific action in the world—you first must envision what it looks like. We all experience the ability to visualize our imaginations in our dream states. The ability to achieve this altered brain state at will through spontaneous imagery can help you prepare to create what you need.

A few hundred years ago, a famous Kabbalist named the "Ari" explained the act of creation using the metaphor of a glass blower. The glass blower begins with an empty mind, then visualizes exactly what he wants to create and holds this image steady. Only then, with the image firmly planted in his mind, does he place his lips on his glass blowing instrument and begin the action of creating the object. This ability to conjure an object in his mind from nothing and then to materialize the image with his actions is an act of will. As the image begins to transform into a glass object, the artist feels excitement at seeing the value and beauty of what he is creating. His sense of satisfaction then motivates him to continue and finish. The imagined object becomes real.

Part III of this book shows how, like the glass blower, you can tap into your creative unified center and blend your wisdom (intuition) with understanding (analytic thinking) to manifest whatever you want to create.

chapter four

The Face of Unity—*Keter*

No matter what his level, each individual has a desire to reach a higher level. It is through this yearning that his soul is formed. But in order for his soul to come from potential to actual existence, he must express his yearning and longing in words. This is by which he will make his desire into a reality and accomplish what he wants.

—NACHMAN OF BRESLOV, *ADVICE: ON TRUTH AND FAITH*

Make my joy complete by being of the same mind, maintaining the same love, united in spirit, intent on one purpose.

—PHILIPPIANS 2:2, NEW TESTAMENT, THE BIBLE

In all the other triads, you begin with the individual opposing faces from the right and left sides of the tree and work up to blending those to achieve balance. In this triad, you do the opposite. You begin with the balanced quality of Unity, the creative source you draw upon to receive inspiration. The "end is embedded in the beginning." The bulk of your work will consist of balancing yourself in the lower realms of emotions and actions. But to do that, you must call upon your upper realm of mind to think clearly about what you want and to determine how to align your emotions and actions with your goals.

On Top of Your Tree

A special feeling comes from sitting on top of the tree of your own life. I will never forget when I was a 14-year-old junior counselor at a special camp for inner-city kids, who never got to see the country. On the first day, I rode with them as the bus rolled into camp, and they cheered with delight at the sight of the lush grass and groves of trees. When the bus stopped, they could not contain themselves and raced to the trees, climbing high into branches, giggling and laughing. The trees were sacred to the children.

From the height of the Tree of Life branches, adults, too, gain new perspectives, better judgment, and greater insights. We can acknowledge our mistakes and appreciate what has helped us succeed, recognizing larger patterns of meaning. When we balance our emotions and actions, we operate more efficiently on all levels and gain access to greater inspirations. We then want to move beyond ourselves and climb toward greater aspirations for our lives.

First, however, you need to assess where you are now, so you can see what you want to change. The upper branches of the Tree of Life clarify the direction in which to channel your actions.

Unity—*Keter*

The face of Unity is the most sacred center within the Tree of Life. In Kabbalah, this center serves as the main switchboard of your creativity, waiting for you to tap into it to deepen your ability to co-create in the world. This center links all parts of the Tree of Life, providing a unifying conduit that activates the dormant potentiality within each of your 10 faces.

Remember the glass blower? He begins with just his wish, or his will, to create action. This impulse to create something material impels him to place his lips on the glass-blowing instrument and to blow an object into being. The Bible says G-d used His creative will to blow air into the nostrils of the first human being—Adam.

Thus, the breath we inhale and exhale through our nostrils manifests the very ethers of our Creator and our creativity.

The center of Unity is like a magnet. Remember the junior high school science experiment in which you spilled iron filings onto a page and slowly moved a magnet across the underside of the paper? When the magnet came near to the iron filings, they magically moved to form a pattern, a new harmonious whole. The magnetic unitive center within your soul can help you bring together the elements (iron filings) of your problems or goals to form creative, whole solutions.

Eureka!

My writing collaborator, Mardeene, writes independently as well and decided to write a book on a topic that inspired her. After writing a few short chapters, however, she felt conflicted, because the book could take any number of directions and the amount of potential material seemed overwhelming. She stopped writing and let the book concept incubate on the back burner of her mind for about a year and a half. The incubation period was perfect timing for our project, because we received the contract for this book and needed to focus on our manuscript!

The speed and ease with which we were working must have lit her inspirational fires. She happily wrote, edited, and worked on several projects about 12 to 14 hours a day. One night, exhausted, she finally went to bed early. She tells me she awoke suddenly at midnight, sat upright in bed with the moonlight streaming in her window and her book solidified in her head. She ran downstairs to the computer and wrote for seven hours. The words literally poured out of her, and she outlined the entire book in detail! She knew exactly how to construct it. All the iron filings had magically moved into a pattern. She felt as if the top of her head exploded, and her whole body tingled for a week. It was an ecstatic experience. Our book also benefited from that inspirational connection.

Biblical Archetype of Unity

Associating the face of Unity with a human archetype is impossible, given that understanding and experiencing something so perfect exceeds our normal state of consciousness. However, the wise ones always used symbols of image and language to help people taste different realms of existence.

The Kabbalists referred to the different branches of the Tree of Life as "worlds." These consisted of four worlds: the lower worlds of Thoughts, Feelings, and Actions as well as a fourth, upper world, the highest manifestation of the Endless Light, called the world of Emanation (associated with the face of unity). Each of these worlds also had a face, which the Kabbalists named. They called the face of Emanation "Ancient of Days." The name "Long Face," which means "slow to anger," also refers to the highest Emanation.

Long Face and Ancient of Days also encompass the wisdom of our ancestors, starting with our grandparents and moving backward through our family tree, leading to the wisdom of the ages. By tapping into the face of Unity we become wiser. Chapter 13, "Drawing Wisdom from Our Ancestral Rings," covers these faces of the soul in greater detail.

Exercise 4: How Close Are You to Unity?

The following exercise will help you assess your unitive will. Put a checkmark next to each unitive quality that is more true than false about you.

1. I can concentrate with total and flexible attention.
2. I love the excitement of creating something new.
3. I experience a deep knowledge of everyday life—able to envision, contemplate, feel, and discuss that which inspires me.
4. My thoughts, feelings, and actions are congruent with one another.
5. I enjoy the pursuit of complete knowledge.
6. I use analytical and intuitive abilities simultaneously.
7. I yearn for spirituality.
8. I use both creative and intellectual abilities, such as those of a musician and scientist.
9. I act with willfulness.
10. I pursue creativity at work and home.

Cultivating Unity

Unity crowns the Tree of Life, unifying all 10 faces of the soul. This unitive center connects to human will. People often misconceive will as a force that tries to control or to coerce into abeyance. Instead, the unitive will of the Tree of Life naturally facilitates the process of personality integration and determined action. This will simultaneously directs and balances thoughts, emotions, and actions—without controlling. Your ability to access your will directly relates to the principle of taking responsibility for yourself and making healthy choices. It enables you to realize you are a self-determined person who can take charge of your leadership process and synthesize your mind, emotions, and actions.

Through utilizing your will, you increase your self-awareness, which in turn motivates you into action. Facilitating the will inside yourself requires active, contemplative meditation. Before attempting to cultivate self-growth through the Tree of Life teachings, you should first learn how to mobilize this unitive will.

You can power up your will through a three–stage process of clarification, intentionality, and mobilization.

Stage One of Unification: Clarification

The process begins the moment you identify which aspects of your tree of life are out of balance. Full clarification results when you understand how to change the out-of-balance aspects of your Tree of Life.

"Clarifying Goals"

Many of my clients use this process to clarify which aspects of their inner and outer selves need rebalancing. Michael wanted to learn to feel and act more loving and secure in his relationships with other people. Cynthia wanted to develop the courage to more freely express herself and to live her life more authentically, reflecting her true self. Jeff wanted to learn to channel his exuberant, over-expansive energy in controlled ways that would bring him peace of mind.

Once you recognize what and how you must change to restore a healthy state of mind and body, you can move to the next stage—intentionality.

Stage Two of Unification: Intentionality

After assessing which branches of your Tree of Life are out of balance, you can start activating your unitive will by asking yourself the following questions:

> How would my life change if my branches were more balanced?
>
> How would I be different if I developed the quality of
>
> _____?
>
> (Fill in the blank with what you need to develop a fully balanced tree, for instance, to be more loving, kind, or giving.)
>
> What value do I place on this quality?
>
> How would these life changes benefit me?

Benefits for Change

Like Michael, you may need to develop more faith through "reverence for your roots" during the intention stage. By evoking the intention to work on developing faith, you transmit negative fear into greater openness and the courage to be your true self in the world. Michael developed his will and with it an intention to open himself to his wife and others and to treat people more kindly. He meditated on what would happen if he allowed himself to be more vulnerable, relying upon the creative source of the universe and other people for assistance.

Cynthia, an extremely intelligent woman, longed to actualize her full potential. However, she had not attempted to do so, for fear of stepping out of her "station" as an obedient child of a family of military officers and as a devoted wife, mother, and teacher. Although she possessed highly developed analytic and intuitive abilities, she had been unable to integrate these two sides of her mind. Her intuition was usually right on, but she didn't trust or act upon it, especially when it came to men. She established her intentions to let go of negativity, to move up in her career, and to attain a comfortable partnership with a man.

Jeff established the intention to use his will to place value in experiences aside from work. His intention also encompassed monitoring his actions to give him more time to spend with his family and to care for himself physically and emotionally. He intended to maintain good health, to improve his relationships, and to smell the roses.

Stage Three of Unification: Mobilization

As you begin stage three, you will already feel positive movements within, prompting you to do the internal work necessary for your next step of growth.

Perpetuating Growth

Michael, Cynthia, and Jeff immediately began to receive positive results as each entered the mobilization stage. By developing his faith and clarifying his goals, Michael rekindled buried dreams, which mobilized him in his job-hunting efforts. His anxiety lessened, and he became more receptive to the process and potential employers. As Cynthia set boundaries with her family and the men she dated, her self-confidence increased. Jeff maintained greater balance between his business dealings and personal activities, taking time for self-reflection.

During the mobilization stage, the main question to ask yourself is: Am I willing to discipline myself to do the work necessary to progress to the next step of my growth? If so, you are ready to tackle one of the qualities you wish to bring into balance using the Tree of Life model.

The Three Strands of the Soul

In Kabbalah, a candle flame symbolizes the three strands of the soul: *Nefesh, Ruach,* and *Neshamah.*

Nefesh, or Animal Soul—the lower black and blue flame—represents the part within us that reacts to internal and external realities. *Ruach,* or Divine Wind—the yellow glow in the middle of the flame—depicts the center of calm, right above turbulence. The *Neshamah,* or Supra–Soul, is the incandescent portion of light at the tip of the flame that disappears into the darkness.

Neshamah signifies the unitive center, which integrates and activates all the potentialities within ourselves. It acts as a catalyst to fire up the positive, balanced attributes lying dormant within ourselves—such as intuition, understanding, love, strength, discernment, compassion, giving, receptivity, stability, humility, trust, responsibility, and faith.

The center of creative will connects directly to *Neshamah*, helping to ignite the creative sparks in all branches of the tree. This creative center also connects with the healer within us that very much wants us to regain our balance and health.

Highly developed meditation enables us to quiet our *Nefesh* (Animal Soul) so we can identify with our *Ruach* (Divine Wind) and bridge it with our *Neshamah*. What does "bridging" *Ruach* with *Neshamah* mean? It is focusing your mind unidirectionally to create a bridge between what you envision and what you manifest. The Tree of Life offers many tools to help you develop this fine-tuned, single-focused concentration. When you can silence the cacophony in your mind and feel the expansiveness within your soul, you connect with your *Neshamah*.

Think of bridging as connecting, or communicating, utilizing a unique language of the soul. Silence is one of the languages to which *Neshamah* responds. Geometric shapes provide another conduit through which to bridge *Ruach* with *Neshamah*. Certain sounds

Neshamah
(Supra-Soul)

Ruach
(Divine Wind)

Nefesh
(Animal Soul)

(Continued on next page)

(Continued from previous page)

and images also help to coordinate your *Ruach*, or unidirectional consciousness, with your Supra-Soul. Just as electricity requires a copper wire with which to channel its energy, so, too, do we need a conduit through which the current of our souls can flow. Meditation plugs us into the source of this current. Throughout this book you'll find a variety of techniques that will help you activate your inner copper wiring to connect your *Ruach* consciousness with your *Neshamah unified center*.

Exercise 5: Meditation on the Three Strands of the Soul

Gently close your eyes and focus on your breathing. Imagine yourself as a radiant flame of light—the Three Strands of the Soul embodied. The opaque tip of your flame stretches upward from your head; the yellow glow fills your chest; the lower black and blue flame shapes your pelvis. Feel the power of the illumination radiating within you, the warmth surrounding you, and your rays of light emanating outward. Intensify your three strands of glowing light, continuing to focus on the inhale and exhale of your breathing. Experience yourself as a source of comfort to yourself and others. When you're ready—feeling relaxed and renewed ,refreshed with new spirit—open your eyes.

chapter five

The Face of Understanding—*Binah*

If you have committed to a study that is worthwhile and do not comprehend a theme of your research, do not fail to continue your application, for in the end, comprehension will come. Does the storekeeper who has sold nothing in one day, fail to open his store the next day?

—IN POLSKY AND WOZNER, EVERYDAY MIRACLES

We can chart our future clearly and wisely when we know the path which has led to the present.

—ADLAI E. STEVENSON

The face of Understanding is associated with the left brain—the rational, logical part of humans. People who overidentify with this side of their Tree of Life, are often extremely intellectual, analytic, and detailed. The upper-left branch of Understanding relates to clear delineation and boundary making. When you possess Understanding, you can break down a subject into its distinctive parts—which is the hallmark of the face of Understanding. For example, the most effective teachers can transform abstract concepts into bite size chunks that help for their students fully comprehend difficult ideas. They can convey the three-dimensionality of an idea, so their pupils can taste, hear, and feel it. When a lecturer or writer accomplishes this, you gain complete understanding of the knowledge you hear or read.

Biblical Archetype of Understanding

Remember, no human archetypes in the Bible represent the upper triad branches of the higher realm. However, in Kabbalah, the face of Understanding represents the archetypal persona Mother. Contrary to popular notions associating the female with intuition, Kabbalists view the essence of femininity and motherhood as the embodiment of Understanding.

The female holds the seed of creation in her womb. The seed can be compared to a flash or spark of intuitive wisdom, similar to getting a hunch about what you need to do. However, the woman also directly experiences the various facets of the seed's development within her belly. In tune with her body, she understands what she needs to help this spark grow into a healthy offspring. Furthermore, after the birth the mother—who assumes primary responsibility for nourishing the child with her milk—understands all the details of her interactions with her newborn. From this point of view, Understanding comprises the ability to separate all the various components of a concept or situation and then to apply that knowledge to everyday life.

You may be thinking, I know several women who are very unmethodical in their thinking and have no understanding of how the real world works! One explanation for this apparent contradiction is that some women have been culturally repressed, which disables them from actualizing their innate abilities of deduction.

Strength of Understanding

Cynthia exemplifies someone whose face of Understanding glows. Since early childhood, she has been an avid reader. The need to live self-sufficiently impelled Cynthia to also develop the capacity to learn about many things. To this day, she possesses comprehensive knowledge on many topics, including gardening and woodworking. As a master teacher, she draws up detailed lesson plans designed to keep the children she teaches constantly stimulated.

Assessing Michael and Jeff's Upper Triads

Michael and Jeff's stories demonstrate the function of the upper triad.

The way in which Michael operated on the level of Mind contributed to his lack of confidence and clarity. Assessment of his status on the upper triad of his Tree of Life "map" revealed he was extraordinarily focused on the left side of Understanding. As a result, he placed absolutely no trust in the right side of Intuition and Wisdom. His left brain kept censoring and editing everything he did or thought about doing, often stopping him before he even got started. His heavy-duty left face pelted him with paralyzing judgmental statements: "What makes you think they'd even talk to you?" "What do they know, anyway?" "I wouldn't like working at that place." And so on. We've all experienced that voice of the inner critic. Fortunately, Michael realized he wanted to loosen up and develop a trust in his hunches and intuition, unshackling the paralyzing chains of his critical left mind.

Jeff was exactly the opposite. His whole tree bent completely to the right, all the way to the ground. On the level of Mind, he ran rampant with his hunches (Intuition)—frequently paying little or no attention to facts and details (left side of the tree). This generated a tremendous out-of-control feeling that panicked him into direct, sometimes reckless, action. Unlike Michael, whose overanalytic mind temporarily blocked action, Jeff was virtually all action. Jeff loved to take action, and often impulsively leapt before he looked. After we assessed his situation, Jeff expressed both relief and fear when I suggested going with him to his office to help him determine where he needed to monitor his actions.

We'll learn more about Jeff and Michael's paths of discovery in the chapters to follow. Now, let's find out more about you.

Exercise 6: What Does Your Face of Understanding Look Like?

The following list cites the varied qualities of a well-balanced face of Understanding. Put a checkmark next to the items that are more true than false about you.

1. I have intellectual pursuits.
2. I reason clearly.
3. I utilize deductive reasoning.
4. I examine things carefully.
5. I enjoy the thinking process itself.
6. I problem solve, generating practical solutions.
7. I am logical.
8. I routinely employ my inquisitive nature about how things work.
9. I constantly seek out deeper understandings about life.
10. I attend to details.

The following characteristics represent an imbalanced face of Understanding. Put a checkmark next to those statements that are more true than false about you.

1. I overintellectualize.
2. I feel emotionally detached.
3. I interact with myself or others in a computer-like, rote fashion.
4. I compulsively perform most tasks, over-attending to the details.
5. I constantly plot and plan.
6. I operate from a matter-of-fact, precise style.
7. I utilize my mind to manipulate my environment, others, and myself.
8. I constantly calculate, trying to predict events for my benefit.
9. I am uncomfortable with emotions.
10. I distance myself from others with my over-intellectualized demeanor.

Cultivating Understanding

Cultivating your Tree of Life begins with developing your face of Understanding. Since this is an analytical process, you should first work on your ability to analyze details. Understanding often serves as a precursor to the expansion of the intuitive mind, which is discussed in chapter 6, "The Face of Wisdom."

Many people who seek counseling believe the psychologist will ask them only about what they feel. Although it is important to explore feelings, it is equally important to understand the underlying belief systems that make us feel the way we do. If you are an overly emotional person, the way to achieve balance is to methodically think about your assumptions about reality. Psychologists call this cognitive therapy.

The Rejection Blues

Philip, age 29, was a chronic worrier, perpetually ruminating and expecting the worst. He also was extremely shy and withdrawn from others. Unable to muster the courage to initiate contact with women, he'd always been frustrated in his romantic relationships. He rarely completed his work assignments on time, hampered by his unfounded inner fear of receiving negative feedback from his superiors.

To balance his Tree of Life Philip had to understand his thinking style, which was getting him into emotional trouble. By challenging his thinking patterns, he realized he typically turned ordinary situations into catastrophic events that may or may not happen. For example, if a woman he liked didn't return his call, he would often sit with mounting anxiety, waiting for the phone to ring, growing sad and sometimes crying, assuming she had rejected him.

He also understood he engaged in absolute thinking. He subconsciously thought, "I must always win the love or approval of others." I challenged the importance of obtaining the love and approval of others—a concept that, judging from his startled look, had never occurred to him. Still, he had to admit that not getting approval from others hadn't killed him or caused him serious harm.

I challenged his thinking on this matter further, asserting that, though he may want approval from others, he didn't need it.

This scrutinizing of his thinking about these issues eventually freed Philip of his inhibition to initiate conversations with women. In a relatively short time, he was successfully dating!

The Perfectionist

Ling, age 20, was a college student with a perfect four-point grade average at a prestigious university. She routinely achieved "As" in all her classes. She sought counseling for relief from unbearable anxiety and depression about the one "B" she had received in a history class, which became unbearable. She couldn't stop obsessing about the grade and was angry with herself and her professor. She constantly told herself things like, "I can't believe I got this 'B'! It's not fair! I should have studied more!" At times, her anger got out of control, especially with her boyfriend, who was threatening to leave because of her behavior.

I discovered Ling was perfectionistic about many things, including her appearance, competing in sports, and her expectations of other people. To balance her Tree of Life, she needed to challenge her unbalanced, absolutist thinking. She operated from the underlying assumption that she and others had to always succeed to be a worthy person.

She came to understand that this predominant mode of thinking made her anxious. She learned to challenge her perfectionism and began to accept her imperfections and view herself as a fallible, but still worthy, human being, just like the rest of us. Her obsession with her grades lessened; the occasional B no longer sent her into a tailspin. She decided to spend less time on achievement-oriented activities and more time having fun and going out with her friends. As she let go of her need for absolute perfection in everything and everyone around her, she also became less critical of her friends, and her relationships improved.

Pain in the Neck

Indira always complained of bodily ailments, the majority of which manifested as multiple pains throughout her body. She carried most of her tension in her neck and shoulders, and would easily become fatigued and grouchy. Consequently, she withdrew from others and spent considerable time alone, trying to comfort her tense body.

Through cultivating her Understanding, she realized the pain in her neck was a symbolic metaphor for the circumstances of her life. Physically, she felt like several people were sitting on her shoulders and riding her back. In fact, she was "carrying" a tremendous psychic and physical load: an elderly but ambulatory father who expected her to clean his house; a friend who leaned on her as her sole companion and chauffeur; a boss who took unfair advantage of her willingness to work extra hours; and a teenage child who constantly borrowed money.

No wonder she could barely hold herself upright. She feared her anger, afraid these people would think she was "bad" if she expressed her dismay to them. She often felt guilty, even when the people deserved her negative, unexpressed thoughts about them.

Like Ling and Philip, Indira methodically examined her thinking process and underlying assumptions about the source of her physical ailments. She acknowledged that her physical pain directly corresponded to her mental pain, which resulted from faulty thinking. She challenged her attitude that others' needs took precedence over her own, recognizing that she had the same rights as the other people in her life. She contested her belief that speaking up for herself would hurt others. With help, she released responsibility for how other people thought or felt about her. This revised way of thinking liberated her, and she initiated assertive and equally liberating actions toward her boss, child, and many of her friends. She was utterly surprised when many of her physical pains disappeared.

She continued to assert herself in other ways. It took a while for her family and friends to get used to the "new" Indira, and she lost some friends. However, she realized many of these "friends" were merely takers in her life, and she worked on developing more balanced friendships. Her teenager eventually adjusted to the new guidelines regarding money. Her boss either paid her overtime or found he didn't need her services after hours. Her husband was relieved, because her incessant complaining diminished and she finally told him what she wanted. He had encouraged her throughout their marriage to be more open about her needs and more receptive to his help. Not only did Indira's new thinking and subsequent actions restore her balance, they also helped bring the family unit back into balance.

Taking Stock

Jeff, an entrepreneur, thought about and analyzed in detail the goings-on at his company, examining areas in which he was directly involved as well as those for which others held primary responsibility. He made lists describing what was and wasn't working, and identified challenges and opportunities he hadn't seen before. In his usual hospitable manner, he maintained an "open door" policy that allowed others to interrupt him at work. However, the constant coming and going of co-workers in his workspace interfered with business he needed to conduct uninterrupted. Co-workers blossomed when he credited them for their work; other times he failed to give negative feedback when he needed to.

As the elements of his work persona cohered into recognizable patterns, he began to use his face of Understanding, without my assistance, to determine when to release or establish boundaries and when to give credit or constructive criticism. He achieved balance by exercising his will and gained confidence in himself.

Deepening Your Understanding

Binah comes from the Hebrew word *Bein*, which means "between." *Binah* reflects the concepts of distance and separation, breaking the whole into disparate parts. Through Understanding, you can distance yourself from what you are studying. The Kabbalah maintains that this process of undifferentiation—moving into something that is differentiated—is how the universe was brought into existence.

The following exercises will develop your left branch of Understanding by helping you to think methodically about your personality as well as your daily life.

Exercise 7: Creative Problem Solving

Now we come to problem-solving analysis, which is useful in developing the analytic mind. Focus on a current major decision you must make and write it down on the top of a sheet of paper. Draw a vertical line down the center of the page, dividing it into two equal columns. Put a plus sign on one side of the paper and a minus sign on the other side.

On the plus side, make a detailed list of the positives you might derive from taking the action. On the minus side, list the potential negatives.

Exercise 8: Developing Your Face of Understanding

This exercise challenges you to think of the various parts of a particular quality you want to develop on your Tree of Life. Remember, Understanding involves methodically contemplating this quality so you can deepen your knowledge of its different facets and then activate it in your life.

Select the one quality (out of the 10 faces of your Tree of Life) you most wish to enhance. For example, perhaps you need to improve your ability to receive. Write this quality on the top of a piece of paper (for instance, Receptivity). Think of all the ways you might enhance this quality in your life and write them down. List all the things you can do to learn to receive from others and to ask for what you need.

These examples of Understanding-enhancing affirmations will help get you started:

The next time Aunt Mary wants to kiss me and give me money, let her.

Even though I always prefer to throw the party, let Sally do it this time and focus on enjoying being a guest.

The next time I need help with house repairs, I will ask my friends to help me.

Tomorrow at work, when John asks me if there is anything he can do, I'll suggest ways for him to help, rather than telling him I'll handle it myself.

chapter six

The Face of Wisdom—*Chokmah*

In the story, "The Duties of the Heart," we read that he who conducts his life as he ought should see with the eyes that are no eyes, hear with ears that are no ears. And that is just how it is! For often when someone comes to ask my advice, I hear him giving himself the answer to his question and that is the way it ought to be.

—MARTIN BUBER, *IN POLSKY AND ROZNER, EVERYDAY MIRACLES*

The doors of wisdom are never shut.

—BENJAMIN FRANKLIN

I have known it for a long time, but I've only just experienced it. Now I know it, not only with my intellect, but with my eyes, with my heart, with my stomach.

—HERMANN HESSE

The Tree of Life teachings associate Wisdom with the right brain. Five thousand years ago the Kabbalists already knew what twentieth-century scientists later "discovered" about left- and right-brain function. The right side of the brain controls intuition and comprises the emotional part of your mind, where creativity originates.

This part of the mind excels at seeing patterns rather than analytic details. It enables you to assemble the pieces of the puzzle into a whole picture. Suddenly, a solution appears in your mind for a problem you've been trying to solve for a long time.

The Kabbalists perceive intuitive Wisdom as a flash of lightning. You know this part of your mind is functioning well when your thinking flows freely. Your mind pulsates like the ocean, receiving one wave after another in perpetual motion, or like an eternal fountain through which energy continually surges upward, out, and around. Each new thought carries seeds of future ideas that form a mysterious chain.

Intuition often comes from deep within the body—a palpable sense you experience in your heart or gut, or a mental image you form in your right brain. Intuition is your "hunch" that something is right or wrong. How often have you ignored your intuitive sense that something was wrong and decided to do it anyway—or decided not to do it when you felt it was right? Later, did you realize your first hunch was the correct choice and that your inner wisdom knew it all the time?

The Tree of Life teachings recognize that Wisdom is very hard to achieve. At times, you must balance your emotions and actions before you can quiet yourself enough to experience what is operating at a subtle level within you, hiding behind your face of Wisdom. Intuition often develops with age. As we gain experience in life or in what we are studying, intuition can spontaneously develop.

Brilliant scientists such as Albert Einstein possess tremendous intuitive abilities. In several accounts of Einstein's life, he acknowledged that discovering the law of relativity actually resulted from an act of intuition in which all the parts he was studying came together in a dream state. He later recorded the details of his vision.

Although intuition sometimes operates in words, it usually speaks in the language of the right brain, through visions and imagination, as it did with Einstein's theory of relativity. In most people, the face of Wisdom is underdeveloped. We can also experience Wisdom, or intuition, through faculties other than imagery and words, though few of us consciously tap into these intuitive sources. We can experience Wisdom as a tactile or auditory pattern, similar to how many artists—such as musicians, writers, and actors—use varying modalities

Understanding Wisdom

In the Kabbalah *Chokmah* represents the essence of a person or thing. You lose the essence of a beautiful mountain lake when you try to describe it to someone else. No one else can experience the mountain lake as you do or choose the words to describe it that you would. Your depiction of the lake, whether in words or even a drawing, comes directly from your experience. *Chokmah* holds all creative potential of the laws of creation. Kabbalists believe the light of *Chokmah* permeates the rest of creation on every level.

Biblical Archetype of Wisdom

The Old Testament associates wisdom with the first emanation of light described in Genesis. When you are in darkness and light a candle, the immediate glow that differentiates itself from the darkness represents *Chokmah* or Wisdom. In fact, the initial glow of Wisdom helps distinguish the Tree of Life itself from its separate faces. This separation of light and darkness depicts the quality of the branch of Understanding discussed in chapter 5.

Wisdom comes in a sudden flash! Understanding breaks apart that initial burst of light into its components. It's like when a photographer, the instant the shutter opens and the light bulb flashes, takes a photograph. At that moment, the camera receives the whole image. Only later, after the captured image undergoes several processes of developing, adjusting, exposing to light, and printing, do we see and understand all the different parts of the picture.

Just as the archetype Mother is associated with Understanding, the archetypal persona Father correlates to Wisdom. The father archetype complements his female counterpart by activating the creative spark. A man makes love with a woman and impregnates her with his seed, which holds the blueprint of unformed life. In the sexual act itself, even the male's ejaculation happens quickly.

Then the woman receives this quick creative spark in her womb, where she contributes her egg and develops the different parts of the embryo into a whole within her body.

According to the ancient Tree of Life teachings, the masculine energy of this biological process carries the intuitive active nature. Cultural influences have driven men away from their inherent intuitive abilities, which their ancestral brethren cultivated through hunting and working directly with nature.

This concept challenges the popular myth that "Men are from Mars and Women are from Venus." To achieve total balance as a human being, each gender must rediscover and renew their inherent male/female gifts. Furthermore, Kabbalistic beliefs hold that both men and women must balance these opposing male–female tendencies within themselves to achieve self-completion, as demonstrated in the Tarzan and Jane story that appears later in this chapter.

Exercise 9: What Does Your Face of Wisdom (Intuition) Look Like?

Review the following statements and put a checkmark next to each quality of balanced Wisdom (Intuition) that is more true than false about you.

1. I have insight into my own and into other people's underlying dynamics.
2. I innately feel things.
3. I act intuitively in most situations.
4. I flow with life's changes.
5. I utilize my hunches to make decisions.
6. I believe in the nonrational.
7. I perceive a whole picture or pattern.
8. I believe we have a sixth sense.
9. I trust in my ability to guess correctly.
10. I experience unusual psychic forces, such as clairvoyance and precognition.

(Continued from previous page)

Review the following list of imbalanced qualities of Intuition, or Wisdom. Put a checkmark next to each of these characteristics that are more true than false about you.

1. I am irrational.
2. I am illogical.
3. My thinking is ungrounded.
4. My conclusions are unfounded.
5. I am spaced out.
6. My life lacks purpose.
7. I feel foolish and act foolishly (irresponsibly).
8. I am faithless.
9. I lack focus.
10. I rely on superstitious ideas.

Cultivating Wisdom (Intuition)

Your intuition gives you a powerful resource with which to change yourself—and you can develop your intuition through the faculty of imagination. In fact, subtle mental images are what guide all of our actions. The active imagination comprises the creative side of your brain, which serves as the gateway to all the other functions of your soul. There, within the creative center of imagination, your mind captures the aesthetics of each moment and perceives things as if you're seeing them for the first time. Developing your intuitive abilities requires exercising your imagination.

Me Tarzan, You Jane

Many couples in marital discord have Tarzan and Jane complexes. Tarzan takes the lead, and Jane follows. Within every Tarzan lives a Jane, and within every Jane lives a Tarzan. These days, Jane wants Tarzan to be more sensitive, and Tarzan wants Jane to be more powerful.

Such was the case of Fred and Karen, who had been married for 10 years. Karen's main complaint about her husband was his lack of sensitivity toward her. Fred, a computer engineer, spent virtually all of his time in his head, whether he was at work or at home. Through his Tree of Life work Fred learned his mind actually consisted of two faces, Understanding and Intuition. However, he primarily expressed only one face—his logical, analytical, left side, Understanding—which bogged him down by focusing on the details of life. Deep inside, however, he felt bored with his job and wanted to exercise greater creativity, which he had difficulty admitting to me and even to himself.

Acknowledging these innermost thoughts and desires provided a good entree for my helping him, because it indicated his willingness to let his imagination wander and to follow new inspirations. He learned to give himself permission to discuss and pursue his hunches for innovations he could possibly activate within his industry. Ecstatic with the results of his efforts, Fred came to life! By mentally locking himself into the role of a subordinate, Fred had allowed his imagination to stagnate, thwarting his creativity.

Inspired by his newfound intuitive work energy, Fred similarly focused on his relationship with his wife. I challenged him to open his mind when he interacted with his wife, allowing in images about how he was feeling and what he sensed she needed from him.

In his well-meaning, clumsy way, he experimented with saying things spontaneously to her, such as: "I sense you need your shoulders rubbed;" "You seem like you're in a bad mood;" or "You seem bored. Would you like to take a walk?"

Karen was shocked! Sometimes his readings of her feelings amused her, because they were dead wrong. But she appreciated his beginning attempts to connect with her in a different way.

The six exercises that follow will help you develop your face of Wisdom. You will learn to intuitively sense things in yourself, others, and your environment.

Exercise 10: Meditating on Objects of Nature

Sit in a comfortable chair and close your eyes.

Follow breathing steps one through three from Exercise 3: "Meditation for Renewing Faith" in chapter 3, "The Face of Faith." Focus on your inhaling and exhaling.

Once you feel relaxed, allow a spontaneous image of nature to come to you. For example, you might envision the sun or moon, a rose or sunflower, an ocean beach or mountain lake, a heritage oak or your Tree of Life. Perhaps you'll focus on nature's geometric shapes—a triangle, circle, octagon, or cube.

As you image this natural icon, tune into its details and subtle nuances. See the colors, feel the textures, and smell the aromas.

Exercise 11: Imaging Moving Pictures

Another way to develop the active imagination is to employ what psychologists call "guided imagery." With this meditation technique, you guide your mind to animate (that is, move) the objects and scenes you envision. The following exercise guides you through animated imaged scenes.

NOTE: For optimum results, audiotape the exercise beforehand and play it back when you do the exercise, or have someone read it to you.

1. Sit or lie in a comfortable position and close your eyes.
2. Imagine you are walking through a lush, expansive field in the country. Feel the breeze in your hair, the warmth of the sun on your skin, and the gentle stretch of your muscles as you move. Smell the grass and the earth beneath your feet, the hint of mint or clover in the air. See the different textures and colors of the environment around you—the sky, the vegetation, the butterflies and birds, perhaps a rabbit scurrying through the brush and an old barn in the distance.
3. As you continue walking through and experiencing this image, ahead you notice a pathway leading to a forest. Imagine yourself entering through the archway of tree branches and strolling through the woods. Notice the diffused light, the shadows, and the brilliant rays bursting through gaps in the tree canopy, illuminating the flora and fauna. Experience the rich smells, shapes, textures, and colors of the environment.

(Continued on next page)

(Continued from previous page)

4. You move deeper into this beautiful landscape until you come upon a crystal clear, calm pond. Gaze at this pond and see the reflection of the sun upon its rippling water and the surrounding grass and cattails rustling in the gentle wind. Feel the wind caress your face and stroke your hair. Breathe in the pungent aromas of this wetland.

5. Now, image yourself sitting on a patch of soft grass at the pond's edge, closing your eyes, and totally relaxing your body, as a sense of tranquillity fills your soul.

Wise Warrior

In her imagery, Cynthia enjoyed envisioning herself as a wise warrior who asserted herself in the world. She'd guide her imaged warrior through situations Cynthia faced in real life, discerning how that humble warrior might respond to the same situations.

She liked that the major prophets were fierce as well as wise. She related to the concept that becoming a spiritual person required embracing the warrior, along with the love and generosity, aspects of yourself, regardless of your gender.

Through her Tree of Life work, Cynthia discovered she tended to over-intellectualize, partly to escape her emotions. She abstracted and compartmentalized, which blocked her actions. These right-brain imaging techniques helped restore the creative right side of her tree, which helped liberate her emotions and actions. She imaged what she wanted, then visualized the action she could take to bring the idea to fruition.

You can use the next meditation to bring together your intuition and unitive creative center to resolve problem areas in your life.

Exercise 12: Advanced Creative Problem Solving

1. Retrieve the list of positives and negatives relating to your pending decision, which you created in Exercise 7: "Creative Problem Solving" in chapter 5, "The Face of Understanding."

2. Sit in a quiet place and place yourself in a conducive meditative state by taking a deep breath quickly through your nose, holding it, and letting it out slowly through your mouth—three times.

3. Review the list of positive aspects relating to the decision you need to make. Consider each component separately, allowing associative images into your mind for each aspect. Actualize these positive outcomes in your mind's eye.

4. Now, one by one, go over all the negative aspects on your list. Again, use images rather than words to envision these negative outcomes in action.

5. Sometimes doing this exercise alone can lead to spontaneous positive problem solving or you may need other exercises that will follow later to further facilitate problem resolution.

Exercise 13: Imaging Your Tree of Life Qualities

Another way to enhance your Wisdom involves fine-tuning the expressions of the different faces of your soul. In fact, you can create an image for each Tree of Life quality: Understanding, Wisdom, Knowledge, Strength, Love, Compassion, Receiving, Giving, Stability, and even Unity. Our minds often form pre-conceived graphic images of the words based on the abstract symbols assigned by our respective cultures and religions. For example, Christianity conceives Love as two doves or the Christ figure. The Buddha figure symbolizes Compassion. Angels represent the quality of Wisdom.

In this exercise, however, (just to begin to practice using your intuition) you will focus on one quality (face) of your Tree of Life, imaging the different expressions of possible images you associate with that face. First, retrieve the list you created in Exercise 8 (under the section "Developing Your Face of Understanding," found in chapter 5.

Sit or lie down in a comfortable, quiet place and return to a meditative state by completing three sets of the breathing exercise.

Review the list of manifestations of the quality you selected to balance. (The example that was given in Exercise 8 was Receptivity).

Now, go down your list, item by item, and envision—with pictures, not words—each of your projected manifestations of this quality through your own creative imagery.

Deepening Your Knowledge

Remember, you can only fully realize Knowledge on the Tree of Life by balancing all your other branches, which you will accomplish as you complete all the chapters of this book. Meanwhile, you can taste your awakened Knowledge by utilizing your unitive center. As you develop both your Wisdom and Understanding upper branches, you will, as a matter of course, tap into your internal, coherent power center. You will sometimes sense your mind opening up and expanding, which can feel exhilarating! As you learn to analyze the qualities you need to gain balance and to employ imagery to deepen your wisdom, you'll feel a magnetic pull within your soul, uniting your thinking and intuition.

Intimate Knowledge, Daat, *reflects the notion of uniting opposites. To love one another completely, both romantic partners must first remove all obstacles from within themselves. Before they can achieve full spiritual knowledge of one another, each must first balance their respective levels of thought, feeling, and action. This involves letting go of their individual egos, thus surrendering themselves to one another.*

Exercise 14, which follows, will help enhance your self-knowledge. First, however, this next story provides a powerful example of all these exercises in action.

Michael, our ex-military officer, used guided imagery techniques to develop and integrate his upper Intuition and Understanding branches, by envisioning what he wanted to do. He'd never really wanted to join the military but had followed in his relatives' footsteps on the assumption that doing so was necessary to becoming a "real man." Michael realized he was by nature a sensitive person, and had always wanted to fully develop his capacity to love. To prepare him for envisioning his goals of rebalancing this aspect of himself, he wrote down all words he associated with his perception of love—openness, caring, children, freedom, giving, and mentoring.

The next step, which proved more difficult for Michael, was learning to relax his body and to release the logic-based grip on his mind, thereby enabling him to work with images, rather than analytic detail. To my surprise, he spontaneously imaged a tree. Through guided imagery, his visualization of a tree opened his heart and elicited new emotions that were taboo in his upbringing. From the roots of his tree, he unearthed the image of his dream for the future. Michael's body language changed from rigid and tense to self-confident and calm. He breathed more deeply, and his shoulders were erect but relaxed.

As he moved through this guided imagery, Michael verbalized his experience:

> I feel as exhilarated as when I fly my plane! I'm way up in the upper branches, and it feels scary up here. Yet, I feel secure in the strength of the trunk, which holds steady, as I sway. It's a little frightening, but fun! I feel love for the tree. This is what I want to experience—total loving.

What sacred qualities does this imagery elucidate? "I am loving, strong, and noble. I am what I am—a tree." If Michael's tree (a shaggy bark, hickory tree) could move, what would be its destination? "I would remain still as a provider for shade and hickory nuts." If the tree could speak from Wisdom of its needs, what would it say? "I need to live on a farm. I crave the excitement of climbing to the top of my branches, where I can experience all that surrounds me—my fellow trees, the sky above, the pastures below, and all the creatures sharing my realm."

Let the Wisdom of your tree speak of your needs and your vision.

> I need to work with children again. Helping and teaching children often relieved my loneliness in the past. I need to teach them the things they need to live independently—the ability to learn, to read, to express themselves. And I need to earn a living doing it. I need to save money to create a farm where children can come to learn and experience new things. I can do this.

Now, visualize yourself taking the actions needed to achieve your vision. What are your first steps? What are you thinking and feeling as you move through your imaged scenes of action?

> I see myself in a classroom filled with children, learning new teaching techniques and building expertise in the instructional arts. I see the children blossom through their learning. I appreciate their frustration with the inadequate guidance in their worlds, for I received little guidance in my family. However, I also know the wonderful experience of receiving strong, clear guidance. I feel excitement and fear about the challenge now resting on my shoulders. I regret being away so long but feel empowered to positively impact the lives of these children, which gives my life deeper meaning. I have deeply missed this experience and relish my return.

During your guided imagery, make sure to let the Wisdom of your soul express both the positive and negative aspects of your vision. Try to end the meditation by envisioning a scene or object that metaphorically depicts the most significant insight you need to gain through your vision. Michael concluded his tree imaging session in this way:

> At some point in the cycle, the farmer must burn the fallen branches, leaves, and natural debris on the forest floor. The fire also eliminates the undergrowth and little scrub trees, leaving more space for the healthy trees. After the forest fire, at first only the grass, and the new carpet of grass looks like an idyllic picture book. Then the rain comes and revitalizes the woods. I guess the moral of all this is: you must go through the fire, burn the decayed leaves and broken branches, to renew the whole forest. I guess that's what I've been doing.

Exercise 14: Deepening Your Hidden Face of Knowledge

We can use the image of a tree, which symbolizes wholeness, to integrate the opposing sides of ourselves. We can also use it to bring together our minds and bodies with our magnetic unitive center.

This exercise combines the problem-solving capability derived from understanding (analyzing) a particular problem with the intuition derived from imaging your Wisdom. It utilizes both of your tree's upper branches as well as the crown.

You may want to again retrieve the lists you prepared in Exercises 7 and 8 of chapter 5. You may also wish to get paper and pen ready for recording your experiences during this exercise.

1. Find a comfortable place to meditate and relax by focusing on your breathing.
2. Visualize a full, perfectly balanced tree standing before you.
3. Recognize that you are the master of climbing this tree. Envision yourself climbing the trunk to your lower branches, then continue climbing through your middle branches and upper branches, until you reach the very top of the tree—the crown, where you can see everything above and below you.
4. Focus on your breathing as you meditate on the quality you need to develop in your life to complete yourself. Recall your list of manifestations that would express the quality you need to balance on your tree of life (in chapter 5, Exercise 8). See each word (or phrase) and say it aloud, then let your mind spontaneously image something that captures the essence of the idea. The image might be a geometric symbol, an icon from nature, a positive memory, or a special person in your life whom you associate with this concept.

(Continued on next page)

(Continued from previous page)

(Remember Michael, who experienced the sweet taste of self-knowledge through imaging the qualities of love he sought to attain. By perceiving himself as more playful and gentle, Michael could reach out to children as he hadn't been able to do with his own children, and to help friends with an open heart.)

5. Experience the solitude and peace of mind surrounding you as your wisdom expands. Gather inspiration from your environment: the sun's warming rays, clouds floating above you, the grass beneath your feet. Feel the sensations occurring within your body at this moment. Open yourself to any experience that comes to you.

6. Experience the deepening and blending of your Understanding and Wisdom, until the serene sense of unity stills you. Then, visualize yourself slowly climbing down the sturdy trunk—through the perfectly balanced upper branches, middle branches, and finally lower branches—and gently step down onto the earth's floor.

7. Sit on the soft earth and slowly open your eyes. Reflect on what just happened to you. If you'd like, write down your experience, which you can use later to interpret its meaning and inspire you to work toward your aspirations.

This sense of understanding and unity may not come to you the first time you meditate. Be patient with yourself and with the on-going process as you learn to balance the different qualities you need on the Tree of Life.

Exercise 15: Using Your Mind to Envision Your Goals

Now that you have been introduced to your whole upper triad of the Mind, how would you describe yourself? At this point, you may find it helpful to set goals for utilizing this book and the Tree of Life teachings to balance your life.

Write a paragraph about yourself, similar to the short profiles of my clients in chapter 2, "Overview of the Tree of Life." How would you describe your basic personality? What major challenge in your life would you like to rectify? What desired or ideal result do you envision for yourself? What branches of your tree must you balance to reach your goals? If you aren't ready to complete this exercise now, just keep these questions in mind as you proceed with this book.

Congratulations! You have finished the first steps to cultivating your Tree of Life—allowing yourself to think analytically (Understanding) and to image intuitively (Wisdom). This will help motivate you to do the additional work necessary to align your emotions and actions toward achieving your desired goal.

Your unitive center—the conduit that illuminates your entire tree—operates automatically when the faces of your Mind are balanced. Moving between the right and left brain, between Wisdom and Understanding, actually activates your unitive center to create something new. Remember, *Chokmah* comes like a flash of lightning, grounding you even as it darts like electricity back and forth between your analytic and intuitive faces. This continual flow of current between your left brain and right brain ignites your creativity, augmenting your ability to achieve what you want.

With your upper triad now developed, you hold the tools you need to proceed with the cultivation of the other triads on your Tree of Life.

part four

expressing your face
of compassion

Introduction: Emotion

As you develop your upper branches of Knowledge—allowing yourself to receive Wisdom and embrace Understanding—you gain clarity and envision your goals. This balancing of your mind kindles the passion within you to actively create a life of abundance.

When you are inspired, your middle branches blossom. You feel motivated to act with intent, and you begin to love both the process and your accomplishments. These intrinsic rewards give you the strength to continually take the steps necessary to move forward. As you embrace love and strength, you experience the balancing of your branches of compassion for self and others. See the diagram.

The famous Kabbalist, Nachman of Breslov, states:

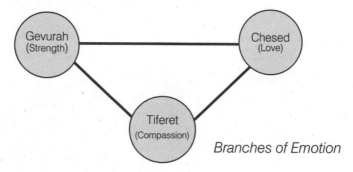

Branches of Emotion

The seed of strength is in the heart. A person whose heart is a friend has no need to be afraid of anything or any person. Such a one can achieve awesome feats and win many hard battles merely through the firmness and steadfastness of his heart. He is never afraid and does not run from the site of a fierce battle. So it is in the service of G-d to understand this well.

Nachman's words reiterate the value of balancing polarities (opposing forces), of combining heart with might. In this section, you will discover how to gather courage to stand up for yourself, fiercely, if needed—like a warrior. You also will learn to use this strength to open your heart and act with compassion—like a lover. In this context "lover" encompasses all human relationships, not just romantic ones, and includes loving oneself. Developing your emotional middle branches of Strength and Love generates the trunk quality of Compassion for yourself and others. This selfless love comes from joy.

chapter seven

The Face of Love—*Chesed*

Spread love everywhere you go. First of all, in your own house . . . . Let no one ever come to you without leaving better and happier. Be the living expression of G–d's kindness; kindness in your faith, kindness in your eyes, kindness in your smile.

—MOTHER TERESA

Love thy neighbor despite all his shortcomings and displeasing habits in the same way that thou loveth thyself with all thy known shortcomings with undesirable ways.

—THE BAAL SHEM TOV
—*IN POLSKY AND WOZNER, EVERYDAY MIRACLES*

By this shall all men know that ye are my disciples if ye have love for one another.

—JOHN 13:35, NEW TESTAMENT, THE BIBLE

Many psychological and spiritual models of well-being depict love in the middle of the heart, or at the center of the chest. The Tree of Life teachings, however, place Love (*Chesed*) on the right branch, the expansive side of ourselves, as you can see on the diagram found in the introduction of this section. Specifically, it covers the right heart chamber, shoulder, arm, and hand.

Have you ever asked yourself why we "feel" love in our hearts? Our hearts register the pulsations of our experiences and with each beat give us the gift of another second of life. Many people do not realize the meaning of their lives until they face serious illness or death. Only then do they understand how much we cling to our life force. When we feel vulnerable, our thoughts turn to love. Who has supported us emotionally? Who would we miss were we to die? The quality of love derives from genuine caring. Loving people tend to be open, trustworthy, nurturing, kind, and interested in others.

The Case of the Broken Heart

The heart provides a wonderful metaphor for understanding the Tree of Life teachings, because like the qualities of the tree, this vital organ expands and contracts. This giving–and–receiving movement between the heart's different chambers is what actually makes our hearts beat, enabling us to live.

The natural rhythm in our heart reflects the middle right and left branches of the Tree of Life. The right side of the tree expands, giving out love; the left side contracts, taking in love; and this steady exchange builds emotional strength. To sustain a balanced flow of contraction and expansion—continually distributing and absorbing emotional nutrients—both sides of the heart must be strong.

The first time I encountered someone having a heart attack was in my early twenties. The person was my father. While I was visiting my parent's home, my father began to gasp for air and experienced sharp pains in his chest and arms. My mother and I knew he was having a heart attack. I remember feeling very frightened at seeing my father out of control, which I'd never before seen. As I drove to the hospital, I became saddened by the realization that in certain ways my father's heart had always been broken. He never allowed himself to receive love openly from my mother, my brother, and me. Like many men of his generation, he felt he had to bolster himself with a powerful, macho image.

My mother often threatened us with my father's strength, because as a woman she felt she lacked the power to discipline us.

For many of us, our fathers became the "boogiemen" we feared. My father, probably like some of yours, often assumed the role of harsh disciplinarian, which sometimes felt abusive. I recall the many times my father was too strict with us and how we felt he never fully understood or loved us.

Then when I was 21 and he was 49, my father suffered a massive heart attack, which scarred his whole left ventricle. The damage to the left side of my father's heart provides a good metaphor for the Tree of Life. Remember, the left side signifies strength. Perhaps his strength and discernment were imbalanced, turning those qualities into criticism of himself and others.

I've observed in my father as well as in many of my patients who have had cardiac difficulties that an emotional transformation takes place after the attack. My father began to mellow. He became kinder toward himself and others, including the rest of our family and me. He took better care of himself, taking more breaks and paying attention to his limits. He spoke more gently to others.

One particular incident from my father's recovery period stands out in my mind. I was sitting next to him as he spoke to his friend on the phone. Suddenly, he placed his hand on mine and told his friend how much he loved me. I began to cry, because this was so out of character for him and he touched me deeply.

He went to the finest surgeons to see whether they could mend his heart, but the damage was irreversible, and they gave him only one to three years to live. My father fooled them all—living another full decade! In that way, his stubbornness and strength served him well, giving him the determination to continue living. Still, the main healing agent was his ability to balance strength with love.

I deeply believe that we all can improve, or even beat, our physical illnesses by cooperating with the natural balance inside ourselves. That is what my father did by trimming back his branch of Strength and growing his branch of love. As a result, he not only lived another decade, but—less critical and more content—he made them the best 10 years of his life.

An expansive quality, Love knows no boundaries. Like the sun, it always shines unconditionally on everyone, whether they are deserving or undeserving, successful or failing, smart or ignorant.

Love is a stable force we can depend on to be there when we need it, sharing its perpetual warmth. Love is selfless. It gives for the joy of giving, loves for the sake of love.

Much of today's literature, song lyrics, drama, and even the news equates love with "passion." This version of love often comes from a place of need and disappoints when it fails to deliver the anticipated heightened states of excitement. In an incredible departure from popular belief, the Kabbalists teach that mature love dwells not in your heart but in your head!

The Kabbalists symbolize love as a fire in the mind.

The Kabbalists say that to love someone is to know the totality of his or her uniqueness, to fully understand and accept that person's weaknesses as well as strengths. Love extends far beyond the physical presence. The test of love is whether you glow from within at the thought of your loved one—even when separated by thousands of miles. Reflecting upon your intimate knowledge of this unique person sparks a warm current that spreads from your head to your heart. And your heart opens up with compassion for your loved one's vulnerability.

Compassion allows you to respond with positive action, giving your beloved what they want or need—which is, of course, quite different from giving them what you think they should have.

With romantic love, this might include, but is not limited to, satisfying your partner's lovemaking desires. There are countless actions that come from caring, and generous lovers give of themselves in myriad large and small ways.

Biblical Archetype of Love

One human archetype of love in the Old Testament is of Abraham and Sarah, an extremely generous and hospitable couple, who invited people, including strangers, into their tents, offering them fellowship, food, and rest. Abraham prepared grand feasts for his guests, even on the hottest days and when he was old and sick. His generosity came not from a need to please or gain favor, but from the goodness of his heart. Abraham and Sarah acted out of compassion for humankind and their wish to perpetuate love in future generations.

Exercise 16: How Loving Is Your Face?

The following statements personify the balanced face of Love. Put a checkmark next to each item that is more true than false about you.

1. I am hospitable.
2. I want to help others.
3. I nurture others and myself.
4. I am generous.
5. I am emotionally accessible and warm.
6. I believe in the intrinsic goodness of others.
7. I am protective of those I love, humankind, and nature.
8. I am nonjudgmental.
9. I am gentle and easy going.
10. I am tolerant and patient.

The following characteristics can occur when the face of Love is imbalanced and causing problems in one's life. Place a checkmark next to each statement that is more true than false about you.

1. I am smothering.
2. I overextend my giving and then feel resentful.
3. I romanticize and idolize.
4. I am jealous and possessive.
5. I self-sacrifice to the point of neglecting my needs.
6. I routinely concede.
7. I am dependent and clinging.
8. I often feel deprived.
9. I am overprotective.
10. I am needy.

As you can see from this second list—which you probably know and don't need me to remind you of—there can be a painful side to love. Yet, the other, more balanced, side to love is joy. When the receiving and giving parts of the equation are out of sync, painful imbalances usually result. When the Tree of Life's contractive (left) side of the Tree of Life receives Strength as its expansive (right) side gives Love, emotional balance—and joy—happens.

Now that you have an idea on where you stand with your face of Love, the rest of this chapter will focus on helping you cultivate this quality within yourself. (You'll work on cultivating the Strength branch of Emotion in chapter 8, "The Face of Strength and Discernment.")

Cultivating Love

In many people, one branch of Emotion dominates, requiring them to first develop the diminished side before they can work on balancing Love and Strength. When an overgrown branch of Strength (left) shadows or obscures the branch of Love (right), you probably need to trim back Strength to give Love more growing room. At the same time, however, you usually must also cultivate your Love branch. For example, one way to develop the right branch of your tree's midsection is to counter the firm parts of yourself by softening your heart.

Late-Blooming Love

Andrew, a gentleman in his sixties, had never married. Although he was very successful in his professional life, he was extremely shy in personal relationships and avoided social groups. He appeared confident outwardly, but inside he felt the pain of loneliness.

Miraculously, he met a woman at the gym, Susan, who adored him. She initiated conversation, because he continued to talk very little. Susan was also in her sixties and had lost two husbands to serious illnesses. In some ways they were perfectly matched. Neither wanted to marry. Both wanted companionship but to keep their independent homes. They saw one another three or four times a week and shared a variety of activities and interests. But Andrew wanted to overcome his shyness. He never thought of bringing his partner, Susan, with him to counseling, and immediately resisted when I suggested it.

Andrew expressed how frightened he was of sharing his shyness with Susan. He felt he couldn't trust others. He was relieved when I talked with him about my shyness. I told him that as a young man I had felt intimidated by people, and that it was the main reason I had become a psychologist. That was a magical moment between us, which facilitated Andrew's trust in our relationship. When he realized he could lean on me for support, he brought Susan with him for counseling.

The Kabbalah teaches that you can experience love through the eyes of the beloved.

I asked Andrew and Susan to sit across from and to gaze directly at one another. Most couples, after the newness of the relationship wears off, rarely look directly into each other's eyes. They often can reconnect through their eyes, by seeing one another with new vision and an open heart. Conflicts often dissolve as they peer into the deep spaciousness of their beloved's eyes in meditative silence. When couples receive each other in this way, it restores the strength and depth of sacred love.

When Andrew looked into the eyes of his sweetheart, his eyes misted and a lump rose in his throat. After taking a few deep, cleansing breaths to unlock the lump of emotion caught in his throat, he spoke to Susan from his chest and heart area, which was also tense. For the first time in his life he wept while looking into Susan's eyes, and said, "I appreciate how you accept me for who I am without pressuring me to be different. You are a miracle in my life."

Susan's eyes lit up. Pleasantly surprised at her partner's spontaneity and candor, she hugged him. Both their hearts opened wide in that moment, enabling them to feel and express their love to one another in a way they never could before. Susan started to cry, which often happens when one person shares a deep vulnerability with the other. Our deepest connections with others occur when we share our pain and joy. Andrew had grown up in a family that was disconnected from each other. With Susan's acceptance, he released his pain of loneliness and isolation and transformed his shyness into self-expression that brought tears of joy.

Self-Love Leads to Shared Love

Sisi, age32, assumed she'd be single forever. Injuries she sustained in a sports accident in her twenties had permanently restricted her physical activities. Convinced she couldn't attract an active mate who would interest her and accept her disability, she was depressed. Part of Sisi's problem stemmed from her absolutist mode of thinking and her inability to set limits on her expansive actions. It had taken a broken body to teach her to slow down enough to receive love. But she also was terrified of rejection—because she was rejecting herself.

Through the Tree of Life map and meditation, Sisi gained the wisdom of self-acceptance. She embraced the parts of herself she liked: her intelligence, spirited nature, and quick wit. We worked on increasing her self-love. As she accepted herself and her limitations, you can guess what happened. A man came into her life who also accepted and cherished her.

Exercise 17: Developing Your Face of Love

1. Write the word Love at the top of a sheet of paper. Now write a paragraph describing your vision of love and kindness. How does the experience of Love feel inside you? Which personal qualities do you associate with Love? For example, Andrew wrote down words such as trust and vulnerability. Don't forget to include the aspects of self-love along with those of both platonic and romantic shared love.

2. After you've written down all the characteristics of Love and what it means to you, close your eyes. Focus on the inhaling and exhaling of your breath, to put yourself in a relaxed meditative state.

3. Visualize each aspect of Love (one by one) that you wrote down, letting the associative images and sensations flow freely. Let memories of this quality flow into your mind—someone who cared about you, your first

(Continued on next page)

(Continued from previous page)

kiss, being hugged by a close friend, being held by your mother or father. Make sure to image self love as well as shared love. For example, remember when you splurged on a vacation, played hooky from work, got a massage, or took a walk in your favorite park.

4. Focus on the sensations within your body. What are you experiencing—for instance, are you warm or cool, tingling or numb, sleepy or energized? Where in your body are these sensations occurring? Don't be surprised if you feel some painful emotions in this process; it may point to work you need to do later.

5. Now, use your mind much like the magnet under the page of iron filings to pull together all the different sensations to form a single image that uniquely symbolizes your face, or quality, of Love. Rachel envisioned herself resting and taking a warm bath when she needed to rejuvenate.

6. Embrace the symbol of Love's meaning to you, then slowly move the image from your head down the right side of your body to your right shoulder point and hold it there.

7. Breathing in and out, focus on this quality of Love resting on your right shoulder and feel it deepen.

8. Slowly move the image to your chest, hold it gently over your heart, and further deepen the image. Breathe in and out of your chest.

9. Affirm the quality of Love as you hold it within your heart by stating, "I have the ability to give Love; I am open to receiving Love." As you affirm this quality, keep deepening this image. Experience yourself embracing the quality of Love and kindness. See yourself emanating this quality in outward action to yourself or others.

10. After you finish meditating on the quality of Love, open your eyes and write down what you experienced.

From Head to Heart

Michael had been operating mainly from the left side of his middle branches (Strength) which included him being overly discerning (judgementalness)—for too long, which had closed off the right side of his emotions (Love). Once he'd opened up to faith and trust, he was ready to tackle the new task he'd set for himself: cultivating kindness and his face of Love. He experienced a breakthrough when he realized he'd been using his protective, aloof stance to separate himself from others. He then was able to open the door to his emotions, to give with greater ease and to receive kindness and help from others.

Slowing Down to Embrace Love

Jeff's hospitable nature was evident to all who dealt with him at work, but he'd been keeping his face of Love hidden from his family. His frantic efforts to keep his roller-coaster professional life from careening off track consumed his emotions. When he realized he himself had set the roller coaster in motion, he knew he could control its direction and speed. Once he took steps in that direction, he felt better about himself and by slowing down at work, he opened his heart again to his family.

Growing Strength to Love

Driven by a need to please, Cynthia had depleted her Love reservoir. People who give too much, fearing they won't get their needs met usually don't get what they need, because they're too timid to ask for it. That was the case with Cynthia. When she didn't get the love she needed and wanted, she withdrew and closed down to love. Her major work at this stage was learning how to love herself, which she cultivated by growing her branches of Strength. You, too, will learn how to do this in the next chapter.

chapter eight

The Face of Strength and Discernment—*Gevurah*

If we could first know where we are, and wither we are tending, we could then better judge what to do and how to do it.

—ABRAHAM LINCOLN

Everyone should carefully observe which way his heart draws him and then choose that way with all his strength.

—HASSIDIC SAYING

On the left middle branches of the Tree of Life is the quality of Strength, which balances the quality of Love. In the Tree of Life teachings, Strength holds equal importance with Love. In fact, you can't be loving unless you are strong within your heart! Strength manifests on the left side of the heart, coming up through the left shoulder point, arms, and hand. Strength creates boundaries for yourself and others. When you're strong, you have a clear sense of your identity. You know where your personality begins and stops in relationship to others. Strength gives you the ability to say no to yourself and to others in interpersonal relationships. It helps you monitor when you're overdoing it in the caring/giving department.

Discernment in Strength

People frequently experience difficulty in love relationships because they aren't discerning enough and thus make poor decisions. They get involved impulsively and then pay the consequences later. Being strong means controlling your emotional impulses and monitoring your giving.

When people receive excessive love, they experience it as smothering and as disrespect of their boundaries. The quality of Strength involves knowing when, where, and how to love, based on the nature of the relationship and the situation at hand. It requires discipline and tolerance. When loving in strength, you discriminate between what's right and wrong for you and for others. It is the apex of discernment. It's trusting yourself to know when to move, when to hold back, when to brake, when to expand, when to stop, and when to leave.

Biblical Archetype of Strength

The Kabbalists cite the story of Isaac and his father Abraham as the human archetype of strength. I struggle with this story as an example of strength, as I am sure many of you do or will as well. However, it is one of those mysterious stories that appears in the Old Testament.

The Creator challenged Abraham to 10 tests of faith to help him balance love with strength during his spiritual journey. We can only imagine the internal conflict he faced when the Creator he obeyed and loved above all else commanded him to sacrifice his son Isaac by his own hand—a supreme test of strength and faith. We do not know Isaac's age, but nevertheless we sense he knows the horror of what is to happen, as his father led him to the mountain top. Yet Isaac had the strength to persevere and follow this sacred command.

The Kabbalists would often see the stories of the Bible as metaphor—many of us need to control our impulses, and at times we all struggle to align our actions with our beliefs. Many of us, like Isaac and Abraham in this story, find it difficult to go against the impulse of human love to reinforce strength. This appears to be what the Creator had in mind. When Abraham proved his love for a higher ideal, that he had the strength to overcome his love of a human being, G-d spared Isaac and substituted a ram.

What about modern life can we learn from this story? Sometimes we must confront situations involving love with great strength. These situations are the most difficult to resolve and force us to establish boundaries within ourselves and with others. Sometimes to maintain balance, our faces of Strength must reign over our faces of Love.

Exercise 18: How Does Your Face of Strength Look?

The following statements reflect qualities of balanced Strength as found in the Tree of Life teachings. Put a checkmark next to each statement that is more true than false for you.

1. I am willful.
2. I am self-disciplined.
3. I am detailed.
4. I think through issues.
5. I can easily say no to others or myself.
6. I know and respect my limits and boundaries and those of others.
7. I am tolerant and patient.
8. I use good judgment.
9. I can be alone for long periods of time without feeling needy.
10. I am independent.

When people are imbalanced in strength and discerning, they exhibit the following qualities. Put a checkmark next to each statement that is more true than false about you.

1. I assign blame.
2. I am self-righteous.
3. I am aloof.
4. I am fussy.
5. I am disapproving.
6. I find fault.
7. I am finicky.
8. I am rigid.
9. I am compulsive.
10. I am stubborn.

Cultivating Strength

The left middle branches of the Tree of Life signify boundaries, knowing limits, and not overextending emotionally. The strength quality teaches us to go back to basics and to allow the serene wisdom of patience in taking time to develop relationships we want. The teachings help us cultivate intimacy and abandon the frantic, out-of-control feeling that often happens when we don't know when or how to slow down or say No. The tree guides us through all stages of balancing love and strength. It shows how to more deliberately receive what we need and what others give us, correcting old patterns of over-giving or over-receiving.

By using strength and discernment, you can more easily decide with whom and with what to get involved. It is often useful to concentrate on your middle branch of strength within your body, feeling it nudge you toward somebody or something that is right for you or tugging to keep you from moving forward.

Face of Strength for Singles

Many single people know they are growing when they end unhealthy or unsatisfying relationships more quickly than they used to. They've come to better know themselves and trust their instincts when they feel things are not heading in a positive direction.

Remember the Kabbalah teachings about romantic partnerships presented in chapter 7? Love comes from "a fire in the mind" that creates love for someone by knowing that person first with our minds, then with our hearts. Similarly, we can create a love of self by knowing ourselves. Stepping back from your heart to give your mind the space to truly learn about the other person, yourself, and the relationship curbs the tendency to love too much or too soon, and to overextend emotionally.

Tradition has it that women are more apt than are men to love excessively. Nowadays, with more women gaining self-confidence and independence and with more men tuning into their emotions, a greater percentage of men also love beyond their means.

This stepping-back process of examining our thoughts and actions involves not only cultivating your middle left branch

(Strength), but also your left upper branch (Understanding) as well. (Chapter 5, "The Face of Understanding," discusses cultivating Understanding.) All the left qualities of your Tree of Life are connected. With analytic self-discipline and strength, you can better understand what you want in a partner and then consciously attract a new partner or develop your existing relationship into the partnership you envision for yourself.

Envisioning the Partner of Your Dreams

George, age 38, believing he always ended up with the short end of the stick, was frustrated by women. He cited a long litany of complaints about his three disappointing marriages and about several close relationships that had failed. Extremely depressed, George numbed his pain by excessively drinking alcoholic beverages. I joked with him that he could have authored a sequel to the popular book *Women Who Love Too Much* (by Robin Norwood), calling his book *Men Who Love Too Much*.

Using the Tree of Life map, he quickly recognized he had been walking around bent all the way over to his right. He sensed (upper-right branch), loved (middle-right branch), and gave too much of himself (lower-right branch) with very dependent, needy women. He saw that his relationships with all of his former lovers hadn't been "intimate" at all; they were more like parent–child relationships, in which he was the parent. He often chose women who were spendthrifts, irresponsible, self-centered, and addictive.

He realized he needed to ascertain what he was getting himself into before getting involved and to discern when to put boundaries on others. He also needed to regulate his giving and monitor what he was receiving in his relationships with others.

He had been separated from his last wife for more than two years and unable to affect closure on their marriage. When he came in for counseling, he painfully grieved this loss. He had difficulty with accepting what he viewed as his failure and with allowing himself to heal. He also still loved many aspects of his wife, particularly that she had been his long-term companion. However, they both realized their relationship involved too much dependency upon one another. As he freed himself from suppressed feelings of sorrow, anger, and fear, he acknowledged and accepted that it was in his, as well as her, best interests, for them to grow and strengthen the left branches of their trees independently.

He envisioned a balanced partner that he wanted to draw into his life. He listed all the physical, intellectual, and emotional characteristics of this woman he wanted to meet. He also envisioned himself as balanced, as well as the balanced relationship he would build with this partner.

He'd never before considered consciously thinking about and facilitating a love relationship. His Tree of Life work helped him understand that most of his earlier decisions had been impulsive and self-damaging, the result of leaning too heavily on the right branches. By the end of his counseling, he was finally able to let go of his wife. He attended support groups and gave up alcohol. He took time to heal himself and be alone before beginning to date women, a positive change for him. He felt more confident in his ability to determine the women he would meet and date. Although he stopped coming to my office for counseling, I believed he was well on his way to healthier, more balanced patterns.

The Tree of Life teaches respect for the sacredness of romantic relationships. You learn to view yourself and your partner as two trees of the same forest, growing side by side but independently, with your roots entwined beneath you. Sharing root systems and similar environments, each tree contributes equally to the welfare of its partner, itself, and the forest at large.

Reducing Reactivity:
Maintaining Your Love Relationships

You feel good with your spouse or perhaps a new special person, happy and balanced. If you are single, you may be delighted or scared to death when you discover this may be someone you wish to stay with for the long run. The Tree of Life helps you hang in there and maintain balance, so you won't throw your partner overboard when the waters get rough. These teachings also help you stay centered in your trunk area. All relationships run into storms. The ancient wisdom of Kabbalah teaches you to relish these storms as opportunities to test your mettle and, if needed, to help you get back on your path of balance.

The major conflicts in relationships have less to do with what people are fighting about than with the way they communicate or don't communicate. We often forget what issue originally sparked the conflict but remain hurt by the way our partners expressed their dissatisfaction with us and the relationship. This happens when the left side of Discernment turns into imbalanced criticism and demands. It can also result from an unbalanced right side that over-gives and lets perceived slights and hurts silently fester until we erupt in suppressed anger and react negatively toward our partners.

The Tree of Life teachings show how to avoid reacting nega-tively during inevitable rough spots in your relationships.

Calming the Storms

Alan, 52, was learning anger-management skills to address a bad habit of flying off the handle with his wife. In keeping with his classic entrepreneurial personality, he always expected things to go his way (imbalanced Strength). He meditated on the left side of the Tree of Life to better discern when it was appropriate to express his feelings and to better restrain his expressions of anger. During meditations, he worked on receiving his wife's anger toward him with greater fortitude. This enabled him to perceive his wife's angry words in a more empathic way. He learned to be more receptive to the anger of the person he cared about (left side) without reacting to it.

During one of his wife's angry outbursts, which lasted for about 10 minutes, Alan just looked into her eyes without reacting—and succeeded in balancing Strength with Love. Finding the center of his trunk and his heart between Love and Strength (balanced posi-tion of both branches), he instead communicated his empathy, saying, "My actions were pretty self-centered. I can see why you're so angry with me. I'm sorry I hurt you. I'll try to listen to you before I overreact." This is a good example of how Alan cultivated his qualities of self-restraint, self-sacrifice, and discernment, which increased his capacity for kindness (right-middle branch) and empathy (middle of chest, middle branches). The blending of love and strength is discussed in depth in chapter 9, "The Face of Compassion."

Blood Pressure Rising

Jolene, now age 43, is a high-achiever whom most people view as a powerhouse. She was very strong-willed and used her discernment with precision (left-middle branch). She married a man who usually did what she wanted, and she held the reins in her household. A successful executive in a growing clothing company, Jolene received reinforcement in her workplace by moving up the corporate ladder. However, just before her fortieth birthday, she started feeling empty, her blood pressure rose dramatically, and she started to experience angina pain.

Her physician advised her to take better care of herself, which she thought she had been doing most of her life. She worked hard, exercised regularly, ate nutritionally, and thought she was a good wife and mother.

Her children and husband joined her for family counseling. Using the Tree of Life as a metaphor for balance, she quickly understood that imbalanced strength and discernment prevented her from fully giving and receiving love.

Her children complained she didn't spend enough time with them, and her husband felt he played second fiddle to her career. During counseling, Jolene uncovered and gained insight into a decision she had made as a child that determined the path of her life. Tearfully—to the surprise of her family, who had seldom seen her cry—she spoke for the first time about her father abandoning her mother when Jolene was a preteen. She recalled being her mother's confidante and hearing about her loneliness. At age 12, she promised she would never allow herself to be taken care of by anyone, especially a man. She closed off a portion of her heart, went on to overachieve in school and work (left side of the tree), and forgot about love (right side).

During one family session, her husband and children ran to her and hugged her, realizing how lonely she felt inside—a transformative moment. She trimmed back her branches of strength to let in love. She used her strength and discernment to balance her time, making it a priority to spend more time with her children and husband. While she cultivated her ability to give and receive love, she learned to use her strength with discernment to achieve greater personal happiness and to continue her professional success. As a result, her blood pressure lowered and her angina decreased.

Exercise 19: Cultivating the Face of Strength and Discernment

1. At the top of a sheet of paper write the words Strength and Discernment. List as many attributes of these qualities as you can think of.

2. Reflect on how these qualities might manifest in your life—that is, how you would experience strength and discernment both within yourself (thoughts and feelings) and in your physical world (actions and interactions). Describe these attributes in writing, for example, "steadfast," "patient," and "think before acting impulsively."

3. Now close your eyes and imagine these different aspects one by one. As images and sensations flow through your mind and body, let memories surface of when you embraced the quality of Strength and/or exercised good judgment. For instance, you might remember the time you stopped yourself from spending money you didn't have, stood up for yourself when you felt a situation was unfair, or watched what you ate when you decided to change your diet. As you envision this, focus on what is happening inside you, the emotions you are experiencing and the physical sensations you are feeling.

(Continued on next page)

(Continued from previous page)

4. Allow all the parts of strength and discernment form a single image that uniquely symbolize this quality in you. You might picture yourself standing erect, exercising, or contemplating a situation before you leap, or an image of Hercules, a lion, or John Wayne.

5. Move this image from your mind through the left side of your body and hold it on your left shoulder point.

6. Breathe in and out, focusing on your left shoulder point, to deepen strength and discernment on your left shoulder, arm, and hand.

7. Slowly move the image of strength and discernment into your chest and heart area, as you inhale and exhale to further deepen the image. Now, breathe in and out from deep within your chest.

8. Affirm the quality of strength and discernment in your chest by saying, "I am strong." Deepen this image inside your chest. See yourself emanating this quality toward yourself and others.

9. Open your eyes and write down what you experienced.

Strengthening Self-Nurturance

Jeff was extremely weighted on the right side of his tree. As the entrepreneur of a successful company, he was remarkably generous and treated people with considerable respect. He made the work environment feel like home for employees and provided ample benefits, luncheons, and other perks. Although he generated the majority of the company's business, he always gave others equal credit. In the process of being so other-oriented and giving of himself, he had neglected his own needs. Although he acknowledged his need to balance his generosity to others with love and attention to himself, he didn't know how to do that. To balance these qualities, he began by making himself less available to others and by saying No more often to others and Yes more often to his own needs and wants.

Conscious Dating

Some years after Cynthia's divorce, when sufficient time had passed for her to begin dating men, she had trouble making the transition. She felt inhibited. She worked a great deal on strengthening her middle-left branches. As she got the hang of it, she became increasingly more comfortable with herself and better able to say No if after the third or fourth date she didn't want to continue seeing that person.

Have you ever noticed that loving, fragile people often are magnets for self-centered types? Such was the case with Cynthia, who was dating Robert, an accomplished professor who always found fault with her. One evening at dinner she'd had enough! Uncharacteristic of her usual yielding stance, she said, "I'm very uncomfortable with how you're being so critical of me. Unless you stop, I'm going home." Robert was surprised. Few people confronted him. However, Cynthia's honesty caused him to think. He listened and changed his style, but she knew he was not the right person for her and stopped seeing him. However, as a result of the positive changes in him prompted by her show of strength, he was more successful in his future relationships.

On Cynthia's part, small successes in developing her strength and discernment, such as those she'd displayed with Robert, gave her the confidence to know she deserved more from a man. She actively visualized who she wanted—a man who was fiscally responsible, independent, unafraid of loving and caring, and noncritical of her.

chapter nine

The Face of Compassion—*Tiferet*

Oh, divine Master, grant me that I may not so much seek to be consoled as to console, to be understood as to understand, to be loved as to love. For it is in giving that we receive, it is in pardoning that we are pardoned and it is in dying that we are born to eternal life.

—St. Francis of Assisi

Compassion automatically invites you to relate with people because you no longer regard them as a drain on your energy.

—Trungpa Rinpoche

Blessed are the merciful, for they shall obtain mercy.

—Matthew, New Testament, the Bible

The Tree of Life teachings see the quality of Compassion as the blend of Love and Strength. The Hebrew word *Tiferet* translates to "beauty." Beauty is associated with the realm of feeling. Experiencing something as beautiful—whether it's a work of art, a scene in nature, or a person who radiates beauty—arouses our hearts. The inherent symmetry and harmony of these aesthetics attract us to them.

Your heart, too, can express its beauty by displaying the mixture of your Love and Strength qualities. The emotional interface between the ability to say yes and to say no, to know when to be loving and when to set limits, is the hallmark of Compassion. For example, one way to achieve the composite quality of Compassion might include seeing the need to synthesize the two qualities of Love and Strength in your intimate relationships. We must learn to care for others and ourselves simultaneously.

If we are to express our face of Compassion, when we must say No, we must encase it within Yes language. We all know that delivering a No in an uncaring way can produce animosity. The compassionate person projects caring through their communication while at the same time strongly expressing No or establishing boundaries. Similarly, while expressing love you must never overlook your own needs, so you can move in and out of relationships without placating and feeling trapped. From this comes true compassion toward yourself and others, knowing nature limits caring through its containers of strength.

When you encounter a compassionate person, you know you are in the presence of a genuine human being. You feel the person's authenticity. You experience an almost immediate sense of trust toward him or her. You know who they are and what they stand for at any given time. A compassionate person possesses the capacity to feel and express the complete range of human emotions.

Biblical Archetype of Blending Love with Strength

In the Old Testament, Jacob and Rachel's love serves as the archetype for Compassion—the blending of Love and Strength. In his earlier years Jacob was mean and deceitful and cheated his brother out of his birthright. He ended up penniless and exiled, learning much about humility and loneliness. Then he fell in love with Rachel. Soon, however his love was tested, and his contemptuous treatment of others was visited upon him.

In accordance with Jacob's pledge to Rachel's father, Laban, he worked for seven years for the right to marry her. On his wedding day, Laban deceived him; hidden behind the bridal veil was not Rachel, but her sister, Leah. So great was Jacob's love for Rachel, he worked another seven years to earn her hand in marriage. He had learned his lesson.

Exercise 20: What Does Your Compassionate Face Look Like?

The following characteristics are representative of a Compassionate person in balance. Put a checkmark next to each statement that is more true than false about you.

1. I am genuine.
2. I am authentic.
3. I am down to earth.
4. I am friendly.
5. I am merciful.
6. I am patient.
7. I am strong willed.
8. I am vulnerable.
9. I express a full range of positive and negative emotions.
10. I feel harmonious with myself and others.

Cultivating Compassion

Compassion is one of the most important qualities, the real power, in the Tree of Life. To achieve balance at the level of Emotion (feelings), you must learn to blend Love and Strength.

Knowing when to give love in which amount and when to reserve love in which amount empowers us. Feeling safe in loving in this balanced way produces a tremendous opening of the heart. You can feel the beauty and vitality of your heartbeat, which, like this quality, is found in the chest, in the middle of the body. The face of Compassion is the central switchboard that all other faces of the human soul must travel through. It means being sensitive to, able to gauge, your energy of openness, kindness, love. Is it too over-whelming? Smothering? Self-sacrificing? Addictive? Dependent? Combining Strength with Love acts as a discriminating thermostat for keeping your openness and generosity in balance. It helps your branch of Love to know its Strength, its limitations, in the world. It does not withhold; neither is it self-sacrificing.

When you arrive at Compassion, you no longer feel compelled to con-tinually prove your love. You emanate a strong, gentle presence. You can say No graciously (with yes language) to someone you care about person-ally or professionally. You also can open up to say Yes after saying No.

Tree of Life and Days of Creation
In the Kabbalah, the days of creation represent the different branches of the Tree of Life. On the first day, the Creator produced Light, which is associated with the branch of Love (*Chesed*). On the second day, the Firmament manifested, depicting the branch of Strength (*Gevurah*). The waters separated from the land on the third day, reflective of compassion (*Tiferet*) because there was a balance between the seas and the earth.

Speech as a Tool of Compassion
Speaking compassionately helps you cultivate the middle branches of your Tree of Life. Throughout time, romantics have known the power of communicating from their hearts. How you express your wants and needs involves, in part, setting boundaries. Expressing yourself as an individual draws on the left face of Strength, although few people know how to do it with love. Practice speaking your truths with conviction and caring simultaneously, withholding criticism. People are more likely to listen and respond in kind when

they feel they are not being attacked. There is power in the blending of strength with love through compassionate speech.

Speech is the vehicle that reveals your feelings. What you communicate and the language you use to express it have as much impact as, and sometimes more impact than, your actions. How you speak can help you become a true lover in all aspects of your life.

Balancing your emotions requires practicing when, what, and how you say what you want to communicate. Your affirming or negative verbal responses can exhilarate or devastate another person. Even language nuances can have a tremendous effect. Similarly, your self-talk affects your internal and external realities. Through balancing your inner and outer speech, you learn to accept yourself and others, which leads to growth of your compassionate heart.

From Anger to Empathy

Some of the best examples of balanced, as well as imbalanced, emotional-based communication are of couples who either live together or are married. It's a shame we often reserve our worst sides for our supposedly best, most important relationships. For example, Enrico and Rosa were at wit's end with one another when I first counseled them. Rosa was experiencing anxiety attacks and felt despair. She couldn't concentrate or sleep.

The frustration in her marriage became more apparent after her husband changed jobs, which took him away more in the evenings. She became very lonely and therefore grouchy. Enrico came home from work to an irritated wife and also reacted with irritation. He, too, was frustrated. He expected his wife to be there for him when he came home after working late hours, and his expectations were not being met. Rosa cried and said she was unhappy, but she didn't dare tell Enrico what really bothered her. She just showed her emotional distress and helplessness. Enrico immediately became angry and said, "Can't I come home to a welcoming house, where I can find peace?" Then Rosa would get angry, saying, "You don't know what it's like to be home all day, taking care of your messes and dealing with the children!"

This kind of verbal expression makes people feel more distant, rather than drawing them together in understanding and compassion, as good communication does. Not only did Rosa and Enrico's words create distance between them, so too did failing to level with one another about what they really were feeling. Many people have difficulty being honest with themselves and with their intimates. When you (phonetically) break down the syllables of the word "intimacy," you get "in–to–me–see." Yet, few of us reveal our true selves to our loved one, because we don't want to feel vulnerable.

Enrico and Rosa worked on changing their communication. Instead of getting into blaming dances with one another, they decreased their reactivity and expressed their real concerns in a calmer tone. For example, Rosa learned to say, "I feel lonely since you've been working late. Could we please spend quality time together?" Enrico responded in a less defensive manner, beginning with an empathetic comment (which he was unaccustomed to doing). For example, he'd say, "You've felt sad since I've been home less. Let's do better. I'm willing to sit down right now and schedule time for you and me to be alone and do something fun." This approach produced very satisfactory results.

Communicating individual needs (left) in a kind manner (right) blends our middle-right face of Love with our middle-left face of Strength. The most prominent problem—and perhaps the easiest one to solve—is that husbands and wives don't give feedback to each other in caring ways. In almost every instance, both are too critical and harsh. The most important step toward improved communication is simply to speak gently with one another.

Little Things Mean a Lot

We cannot all do great things; we can do small things with love.
—MOTHER TERESA

Resentments often grow when both partners in an intimate relationship believe they are giving to the relationship but their giving is actually self-centered. Ben and Beatrice often argued about feeling deprived and unloved by the other. When challenged to name ways in which she wanted to be loved, an inquisitive look came over Beatrice's face, and she stated that no one had ever asked her that. She had to think hard to envision her symbols of love. Eventually she said, "I loved it when he called me during the day to ask how I was or surprised me with a hug from behind. He just doesn't do that anymore. Those gestures kept me in love with him."

It is the small daily things we do for one another that bind relationships. Ben was upset that Beatrice had never visited his family. He was more family-oriented than his wife. He was secretly hurt by his belief that Beatrice felt superior over his family. She often stated she had nothing in common with them. His symbol of care consisted of his requesting she attend one family gathering a month.

They compromised on their differences in the amount of time they would spend with his family. To her surprise, the more she let in his family, the more her husband's nephews and nieces wanted her to play board games with them, and she began to open her heart. Consequently, he, too, more frequently hugged her spontaneously and expressed his feelings of love and gratitude. This blending of love and strength produces compassion, which usually occurs when partners clearly articulate and work out their individual needs, which inspires mutual love.

Bringing Compassion to Your Life Through Compassion for Yourself

Sisi, the sportswoman who overextended herself and became disabled, needed to develop her left-middle face of strength and recognize her limitations. She needed to learn to say no to herself and others with regard to what she could do physically.

Part of increasing her Strength involved increasing her self-love (right–middle face), which also included being compassionate toward herself. This helped her to cultivate the quality of Strength and self-restraint (left-middle face).

When she succeeded in appreciating herself, handicap and all, so did others—including Franklin, a caring man who came into her life and looked beyond her physical challenges. She was delighted to attract a kind and discerning man who, like Sisi, was also physically active. She was even more delighted when he asked her to marry him.

Intimacy and Sex

Some couples come into counseling focused on their genitals, with one or both spouses claiming dissatisfaction with their sexual relationship. The word intercourse means communication, and there are different types of communication. Sex is nonverbal communication. When a couple's emotional communication is lacking, it interferes with their sexual connection.

Intimacy comes from knowing someone. Some people interpret the Bible's depiction of when Adam came to "know" Eve as sex. But think about the association of the words "to know" with sex. Knowing comes from the mind, remember?

Sexless Everywhere

Lois and Harry sought counseling because Lois had no desire for sex. They also wanted to see change in each other. As part of their Tree of Life couples work, they did a communication ritual that encouraged them to communicate with one another—sharing new information each day or at the end of a week. Even though they felt close with one another, they couldn't physically connect.

The next phase involved massaging one another, each week gradually getting closer to their erotic areas. During the massages, they verbally communicated with one another about how it felt to be massaged by their spouse. At that point, couples who have not been having physical relations often initiate sex spontaneously.

Lois and Harry found the balance between their verbal and nonverbal communication. Rebalancing the give and take of speech as well as physical actions creates more stability and blends heart with sexual yearning through physical touch.

Family Root Systems

Family members are like trees closely linked in the forest. Each tree supports the root systems of the trees surrounding it. The roots of entwined trees exchange nourishment between each other. They also realize that all it takes is one imbalanced tree to infect all other root systems. Through the knowledge that the root systems of the human family are all interconnected, we understand that no person's needs take precedence over another person's needs. Everybody gets equal share in the same space.

One unstable person or sapling in the family can serve as a valuable thermostat. This family member's distress or acting out signals the family's need to realign and to strengthen their root system.

The Family Barometer

Barry, age 14, came to therapy with his mother, father, and 12-year-old sister. Barry's mother stated he was a disruptive force in the household and had no respect for her or his sister. He often disobeyed and cursed at his mother.

During one session, Barry disagreed with his mother about curfew and, sure enough, cursed at her right in front of me. All the while, the father remained silent. When asked why he let his son talk to his wife in demeaning ways, the father lowered his sunglasses over his nose, stared at me, and said, "Because she deserves it." This so-called symptomatic child was the father's mouthpiece toward his wife. In fact, I commended the child for his disruptiveness, because it had brought his family to counseling. It allowed his father to learn to express himself to his mother, who was ready to get divorced.

The father had never dealt with his differences with his wife. He went along with whatever she wanted in the name of "love." He thought love meant never fighting, and he ended up placating. When he needed to say no, he didn't communicate his wishes. As he learned to communicate his needs to his wife and received what he needed, he felt more compassionate, which opened up his heart toward his wife. As they balanced their communication, they both were better able to flow with their love and strength. Barry became more comfortable and much less disruptive.

Sometimes Love Means Relaxing Boundaries

I consulted with a single mother of four, with a 13-year-old daughter, Jeannine, who was bright, inquisitive, witty—and extremely rebellious. She frequently did the opposite of what she was asked to do.

When the family marched into my office, I was startled. All of the kids were dressed alike, as if in uniform: brown pant suits with buttoned vests, brown socks, brown shoes, and white shirts. Only one differentiated herself from her siblings. Guess who it was? Our friend, Jeannine. Her vest and jacket were pointedly not buttoned up, her blouse was a black and brown jungle print, and black panthers dangled from her earlobes.

During the session, it became clear the mother was the switchboard in the family. When I talked with each child about what she or he wanted to see changed in the family, each would always hesitate and look at their mother, Barbara's, eyes. Her presence was overwhelming. The children had to physically move their chairs away from her to talk with me.

When I later worked individually with Jeannine, a creative child, she drew a very telling picture of a horrific-looking monstrous figure, hovering over a city and dropping bombs all over the place. The monster was clearly female and greatly feared. It reminded me of a Godzilla movie in which the huge monster stomps on people. Guess who this "monster" represented in her mind?

After getting to know Barbara, I saw she was extremely loving in her heart toward all her children. You could feel the genuine care she felt when she cried about how their father had left them and she had to take command of her life and theirs without support.

Even after the divorce, the father obviously continued to wield a strong influence on the family, and there was constant conflict. She described their household while he still lived in the house. When her husband came home from work to a disorganized house, he exploded and screamed at her for not keeping things in order. He was also intolerant of the children and attacked them for not keeping their rooms clean.

One time, after the divorce, he took issue with her wanting the children to have a curfew. He got angry and accused her of overprotecting them. In some ways, he had a point. However, in that particular context, she had a right to be concerned. Their house bordered on a neighborhood that was dangerous for teenagers because of gang activity. This divorced husband and wife needed to find a balance they had never achieved while married.

The mother prided herself on keeping together her family and on how her children were, for the most part, respectful, caring, and loving—except, of course, Jeannine. The mother felt especially close toward this child and couldn't understand why she was rebelling and misbehaving.

I became very interested in this family and did a home visit. I couldn't believe what I saw when I walked through the door. Everything in the house was in perfect order and perfectly matched everything else. It seemed as if the ghost of the father still resided there. Because Barbara was extremely anxious and felt out of control, she needed to control her outer surroundings to give her some sense of inner stability.

She worked hard for long periods of time on love and strength. She was far out of balance on the left-middle face of strength of her tree, which rendered her overly self-effacing, self-controlled, and critical of herself and others, including her children. Her boundaries in the world were too rigid. Her fear of losing control prevented her from nurturing her daughter's individuality, which she actually admired.

Barbara's children were her total world. She had no serious outside connections with others. She worked on letting go of control and practiced kindness and openness to people outside the family. Her heart on the right side of the tree started to soften. Eventually, with encouragement, she connected with other single mothers in the community. Over time, she blossomed, began to date, and built a life for herself, which freed her children. She stopped obsessing about her home and children, who became more relaxed. Jeannine rebelled less, although one of her strengths continued to be her obvious individuality.

Sugar Smothering Love

One very sweet but extremely nervous grandmother could no longer take the constant arguments with her 12-year-old granddaughter, who was diabetic. In this unique situation, three generations of women lived in the same house—the grandmother, her daughter, and the 12-year-old. Many of their arguments were about the child taking her insulin, which she needed to do daily. When the family smothered her with their well-meaning suggestions, the young girl often then had a diabetic crisis and was taken to the hospital.

During the first consultation, everybody talked for everybody else. The mother answered for the grandmother; the 12-year-old answered for the mother; the grandmother answered for the child. It was as if the family were one gigantic mass with no clear boundaries between family members.

The daughter's diabetes was unstable because when she felt her identity was not being respected, she often rejected taking the medication. The boundaries were too rigid. The mother and grandmother had the same kind of enmeshed relationship as the child and mother, in which the grandmother always told the mother what to do. This kind of behavior in a family is often labeled as caring and loving (right-middle face). However, loving that moves toward smothering is a damaging kind of love. It inhibits the left face of strength and discernment from developing in balance with care and love. This extreme order, conformity, and overinvolvement for the sake of "love" does not honor individuality and is not truly loving.

This family's main issue was that the child was overprotected. Her mother and grandmother did not respect her autonomy. A major breakthrough occurred when the daughter was empowered to talk with her physician about how she could administer her own insulin shots to herself. She learned to do this, and her diabetes became more regulated, requiring fewer trips to the hospital. The family also learned to balance their love by decreasing the "sugar"—their overprotective responses. By respecting each other's individual strengths and autonomy in a more caring way (balancing left branches), they let in compassion.

For families to survive in a healthy manner, each of the trees must occupy their individual space in the family forest, where root systems gently connect with each other. Densely entangled tree roots can throw off the whole ecological balance of the forest family, resulting in illness and discord.

Exercise 21: Cultivating the Face of Compassion

In this exercise, you will bring together your images of Love and Strength, integrating these qualities within yourself.

1. Focus on your breathing.
2. Visualize the image of love and kindness that you already experienced. Perhaps you see yourself smiling or wearing a soft glowing face, or see two doves kissing.
3. Once you've locked this vision clearly in your mind, bring the image down the right side of your body and move it to your right shoulder point. Gently hold it there, inhaling and exhaling as you focus on the right shoulder point embracing the quality of love and kindness. Let this emanation flow from the focal point of your shoulder through the right side of your body, your right shoulder, right arm, and right hand. Continue to hold the image of love on the right side of the middle of your body as you again visualize your symbol of strength and discernment. Perhaps you picture a large rock or a powerful, but cautious, lion.
4. Once this image of strength appears clearly in your mind, move it down the left side of your body and hold it at your left shoulder point.
5. Deepen the quality of strength and discernment as you inhale and exhale. Move the image from your left shoulder point through the left side of your body, your left shoulder, left arm, and left hand. Perhaps you experience the quality of the lion; you feel yourself with greater confidence and agility.

(Continued on next page)

(Continued from previous page)

6. Hold the images of both love and kindness on your right shoulder point and strength and discernment on your left shoulder point. Focus on your breathing as you deepen the images.

7. Very slowly and simultaneously bring these images into the middle of your chest. Let them blend into another single image composed of them both. As you hold together these two combined qualities (the doves and the lion), let a new image emerge that melds these qualities (perhaps a strong but gentle dog, such as a St. Bernard who rescues children). Tune into your ability to experience harmony and compassion. Let new images appear; when you experience a particular image more deeply, latch onto it and go deeper still into that one image representing both love/kindness and strength/discernment. Other examples of images that blend Love with Strength might be the powerful currents of the ocean gently receding from the earth or of the Christ or Buddha figures.

8. As you hold this blending of qualities in your chest, breathe in and out. Affirm to yourself: "I am harmonious in my emotions. I am compassionate. I am loving and kind, strong and discerning." Deepen the sensations occurring within your chest as you inhale and exhale. Notice the sensations you feel in your body as these qualities blend together.

9. When you are ready, let the images dissipate, return to yourself, and write about this experience.

This section has focused on the realm of Emotion. You have learned to assess where you are on the middle branches of your Tree of Life. You now understand how to cultivate the branches of Love or Strength you want to grow and how to blend these branches to balance yourself.

Michael and Cynthia Blend Love with Strength

Cynthia discovered imbalances on both sides of her emotional tree, which she needed to integrate. Her left side of Strength was overly judgmental of herself and others. Conversely, she swayed too far to the right trying to please and giving out too much. She did not know how to employ Strength in Love. As a child, she had used her reclusive reading to deal with her loneliness. She'd had little experience in the real world with expressing emotions in relationships.

Boundary issues can be difficult to grasp, especially for caretakers, such as mothers, on whom many others typically depend for nurturing and stability. Cynthia worked at being more direct with her adolescent daughter and others. She finally said things like, "No, I cannot leave work to bring you the homework you forgot. I'm confident you can remember your homework in the future."

Michael is heavily overbalanced on the left side. He is overly critical of himself and others, which led him to perfectionism and disappointment and to making poor judgments about himself and others. He realized his depression and marital problems stemmed partially from his defense of needing to appear in control, which translated to others as arrogance and kept him separated from people. His wife complained that he lectured her too much, sounding like a professor. That attitude isolated him from his family as well as from the people he needed to give him a job. He worked on developing his kindness, generosity, and openness. He achieved this by initiating conversations with others and taking interest in their lives. He then enjoyed gradually increased success in the way others perceived him.

part five

building your face
of stability

Introduction: Action

If you've been cultivating the upper and middle branches of your Tree of Life (part three, "Reaching for Knowledge," and part four, "Expressing Your Faces of Compassion"), you have already strengthened your lower branches of Stability. We gain stability by aligning our upper branches of Knowledge, increasing our self-awareness, and understanding our goals and aspirations. We can also augment Stability by balancing our middle branches—opening our hearts, inspiring us to care, and expressing compassion for others and ourselves. We further increase our stability by developing the fortitude to align our actions with our thoughts and feelings.

Now it's time to work directly on the lower branches of your Tree of Life: your face of Stability. The lower triad's purpose is to produce impeccable action in the world. Renewing our roots and synthesizing our mind and emotions activates a need to respond and to take responsibility.

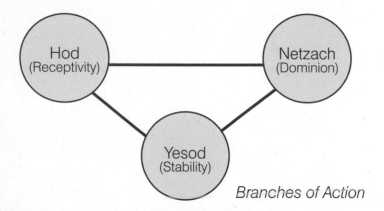

Branches of Action

The right face is Dominion, *Netzach*, which translates to "victory." We achieve victory, or success, by taking conscious control in directing our energies. The left face is Receptivity—*Hod*, which translates to "splendor." We experience splendor in the awe and joy of creating something. Psychologically, it is the ability to stand back from your actions and to let yourself experience the fruits of your efforts. The balanced face in the middle of your lower branches is Stability, *Yesod*.

chapter ten

The Face of Dominion— *Netzach*

For the things we have to learn before we can do them, we learn by doing them.

—ARISTOTLE

Action is the product of the qualities inherent in nature.

—BHAGAVAD GITA

Sow much, reap much, sow little, reap little.

—CHINESE PROVERB

You will soon break the bow if you keep it always stretched.

—PHAEDRIUS

The Tree of Life teachings correlate the face of Dominion with taking control and directing your actions toward specific goals. This quality perpetuates movement or leadership in a particular direction. When you engage your Dominion, you tenaciously persevere, asserting yourself as the ruler of your own domain.

Dominion focuses your mind on achieving what you set out to accomplish, allowing no distraction to deter you. It is the quality directly connected to the forces of growth.

Once a branch starts to develop, it continues to grow in the direction it is reaching toward.

Although taking dominion in your life might seem to be a bit self-centered, this branch actually relates to giving of yourself. Dominion is located directly beneath the emotional branch of Love. The key difference between the Dominion and Love branches is best summed up in the adage actions speak louder than words. The branch of Love in the middle Compassion triad reflects an emotional attitude we express through either (or both) non-verbal gestures or verbal communication. The face of Dominion puts these emotional qualities into action.

Biblical Archetype of Dominion

The Old Testament represents the quality of Dominion in the archetypal figure Moses. With Moses's direct connection to the Holy Power above coupled with his tremendous will and tenacity, he leads the Israelites to deliverance, despite their constant rebelling. Moses was a man on a mission!—rooted to his goal of keeping the Israelites connected to the wisdom of the Creator.

The Walt Disney film *The Prince of Egypt*, (the frequency with which I mention Disney movies stems from living with my six-year-old daughter), clearly depicts Moses's mission. He first encounters G-d through the burning bush, which talks to him and says, "I Am that I Am." Sound familiar? (Refer to the Tetragrammaton in chapter 3, "The Face of Faith.") G-d sent Moses with his brother, Aaron, to Egypt to stop the Pharaoh's oppression of the Israelites. We all remember the exciting story of Moses predicting the 10 plagues, the Egyptians pursuing the fleeing Israelites, and Moses miraculously parting the waters of the Red Sea to allow the Israelites to escape.

While Moses meditated on top of Mt. Sinai for 40 days and 40 nights, receiving the Ten Commandments, the Israelites started rebelling against G-d by worshipping the golden calf, a symbol of idolatry. Moses loudly admonished the people and broke the stone tablets on which he'd written the commandments, but he pleaded with G-d for forgiveness on behalf of the Israelites. Moses persevered and successfully guided his people to the Promised Land. Moses represents impeccable leadership, the core of Dominion.

Getting in Gear

Michael ascertained that his face of Dominion, like his faces of Strength and Understanding, leaned too far to the left. After he had retired from the military, the "commanding officer" of his left side continued to demand perfection and to stifle inspired and compassionate action on his right side. This drove him to act compulsively and prevented him from securing civilian employment.

People who are insecure on the level of action usually respond by either withdrawing or being overly controlling. Michael had felt secure in his familiar, structured military career in which he encountered few risks. However, he struggled against withdrawing when he faced job-hunting in a strange, new world that at times felt hostile to him. At home, on the other hand, in a situation with which he was familiar, he became over-controlling with his wife and children. He was miserable but did not know how to change. He was determined to stop dominating and oppressing his family and himself. Accordingly, he wanted to take positive action toward bringing balance and openness into his life.

Exercise 22: What Is Your Expression of Your Face of Dominion?

The following are attributes of people who exhibit the balanced quality of Dominion, or assertiveness, in their daily lives. Put a checkmark beside each statement that more accurately than not describes your modus operandi in the world.

1. I am goal oriented.
2. I often take the lead in facilitating events in my daily life.
3. I assert myself.
4. I possess and utilize my leadership ability.
5. I am tenacious.
6. I exert tremendous energy and enthusiasm toward making things happen.
7. I focus on getting the job done.
8. I have an above-average capacity for concentrating on a specific action.
9. I am ambitious.
10. I pursue excellence.

Imbalanced Dominion

The positive aspect of taking control of your dominion can easily turn into imbalance. For example, both men and women can be excessively domineering in their relationships.

Dominant people often impose their values of right and wrong without sensitivity to the needs of others. This can happen in marriage when an overly controlling person doesn't receive and/or reciprocate love in the way the other would like, which hurts the giving partner. Many times one partner's symbol of love differs from the other's symbol. To give from a balanced position, we must empathize with others, which correlates with the left branch of Receptivity, as discussed in chapter 11, "The Face of Receptivity."

Domination, whether in a relationship with a spouse, friend, or child, can also emerge as suffocating over-involvement. If anyone has ever smothered you with overbearing devotion, you can probably see how this style of "caring" can be as damaging a form of abuse as neglect. Overprotective people rob others of the opportunity to develop their self-confidence, individuality, and independence.

Another imbalanced action of domination is compulsion—the inability to stop impulsive actions. The compulsivity might lead to excesses in such common activities as working, eating, or surfing the Internet. It can surface in more innately destructive compulsive activity, such as addictions to drugs, gambling, and sex. Extreme, disabling compulsivity usually indicates the need for a psychiatric/psychological evaluation to determine the need for medical treatment together with traditional psychotherapy.

Exercise 23: How Stable Is Your Dominion?

The following personality traits indicate an extreme imbalance in a person's Dominion. If your character leans more heavily toward these negative qualities than the positive ones in Exercise 22, your face of Dominion is imbalanced, indicating the need to strengthen your branch of Receptivity.

Put a checkmark next to each of the following statements that is more true than false about you.

1. I want to control everything.
2. I tend to dictate the actions of others.
3. I am tyrannical.
4. I bully others.
5. I am overbearing.
6. I am impulsive.
7. I am intolerant.
8. I am self-centered.
9. I am arrogant.
10. I am overprotective.

Genesis of Dominion
The branch of Netzach *(Dominion) reflects the fourth day of Creation, when the Creator set in motion the celestial elements. These heavenly objects are bound by strict, undeviating laws. For millions of years, the Creator has used these axioms to control how these elements act.*

Cultivating Dominion: Taking Action

People who embrace the quality of dominion are ready to work toward changing something in the present. They want to create a specific result that positively influences others or themselves. Action-oriented people focus on a tangible goal. This objective may comprise enhancing one's relationship with a spouse or friends, increasing one's productivity and efficiency at work, improving one's job satisfaction, or in some other specific way benefiting others or oneself. Dominion is found in the right pelvis, right leg, and right foot—the location from which you put your right foot forward.

Growing Up Hard
Most people who seek therapy must deal with the issue of Dominion, usually because they don't assert themselves enough. I first counseled Gary, a young man of 24, when he was six years old and his mother brought him because he was very shy. His father had left the family when he was only two, and like many single mothers, his mother overprotected her son. Gary and his mother were like two peas in a pod. In single-parent families, mothers sometimes depend too heavily on their children for social interaction, which was the case with Gary and his mother. One of his complaints as a six-year-old child was that others often called him a "mama's boy."

Little Gary was eager for a respite from his mom. He was clearly glad to be around a man and enjoyed it when we played board games together. During the six months of therapy, he learned to stick up for himself when bullies antagonized him. By reducing his shyness, he was able to stand his ground when kids insulted him. Kids often insult their peers and usually target the most sensitive ones. Role-playing taught Gary to react more assertively when other children teased or called him names. He'd retort, "I heard there is something wrong with kids who make fun of other kids!" They backed off. He felt proud of himself, and it boosted his self-confidence.

Twelve years later, when he was about 20, Gary's mother called me again. Gary was stagnating and floundering. When I saw him, I instantly recognized him: although he was bigger, he had the same sad, shy eyes. He felt alone and depressed. He felt so painfully alienated from his peers that he had dropped out of college.

Through his Tree of Life work, he slowly began to take control of his life and to branch out. He re-enrolled in school. He developed the quality of patience while he simultaneously built his face of Stability. I assured him that some trees mature more slowly than others, but all trees eventually sprout in full splendor. He learned of many examples of people who, like some trees, were late bloomers. He mapped out a strategy to slowly take dominion around school.

He had always wanted a girlfriend but didn't know how to initiate contact. He started by simply smiling at the girls around him. To his surprise, they smiled back! He was a good-looking guy, but self-conscious. The next growth step was to say hello to a girl to whom he wasn't attracted. Next, he initiated easy conversation with girls who didn't threaten him, asking them how they were doing and how they liked their classes. Eventually, he moved on to girls he was attracted to, and lo and behold, a girl he liked asked *him* out! This boosted his self-confidence 100 percent. I always tell young men that the best therapy for shyness is holding a young woman's hand, which certainly worked for Gary. He went on to finish college and got married.

Branching Out at Work

Ken, a whiz at expanding his role inside his company, provides a good example of expanding the right side of Dominion. There wasn't anything Ken wouldn't tackle at work. He created multiple roles for himself at his company—from technical support to hands-on manufacturing operations, interviewing new employees, and reorganizing the physical plant. What he needed help with was taking the next major step in his career. He realized that the prospects for his future were declining at his current place of employment. Tapping into his upper faces of inspiration, he identified a number of industries to which he could apply his considerable talents and experience. He increased his circle of influence, networking with people outside his current realm. He then used his lower face of action to successfully expand into a new job as operations manager of several diverse operations within a new company.

Listening to Your Gut

People who struggle with imbalanced Stability can possibly develop physical ailments with their colon or other parts of their lower bodies. Sharon, age 27, suffered from colitis. As far back as she could remember, she had experienced stomach pain. Easy going and generous, Sharon was loved by many and had a large social network. Guests stopped over to her home nearly every day of the week. She was exceptionally giving, kind, and hospitable to others. She typically yielded to everyone's needs and was everyone's best friend—but her own. She was tuned in to others but tuned out her needs. She suffered from anxiety, but no one knew, because she always wore a smile.

Internally, she resented her friends. Many people with colitis have mixed feelings about their relationships with others. On one hand, they very much want to receive love; on the other, they resent the people they are dependent upon or who cling to them.

She needed to balance her positive inclination of being receptive to the needs of others with taking more control over her dominion, starting with her own home. Very gradually, she set boundaries, using her middle-left face of discernment, and asserted herself at the level of action. She learned to do what she wanted to do rather than what others expected of her. She clearly understood her lack of assertiveness was related to her colitis. As she strengthened her faces of Dominion, her colitis decreased. She learned to say No more often when friends wanted to come over and it wasn't convenient for her. She spoke up with her husband, expressing her desire to go out with him alone. She allowed time to develop her career.

Exercise 24: Cultivating Your Face of Dominion

The following steps can help you balance the level of action with the quality of dominion to assert yourself in moving toward your goals.

1. Write the word Dominion at the top of a sheet of paper and list the attributes you need to acquire or hone to better control your life. Remember that the ability to take control is associated with leadership. Dominion does not mean domineering and over-controlling. It simply means asserting and directing your actions to reach a goal that benefits others or yourself. For example, Sharon wrote, "I want to say no, spend more time alone, and go on dates with my husband."

2. Now close your eyes and imagine all these different aspects, one by one, manifesting in your life. Allow images and sensations to flow through you. Let memories of witnessing this quality previously in your life emerge. Remember the times when you stood up for yourself, or if that is difficult, recall someone you admire standing up for himself or herself. Experience the emotions you feel when asserting yourself.

3. Focus on what is happening within you as you imagine this quality. What are you experiencing? Focus on all these sensations—visual, tactile, emotional, auditory, spiritual—as you deepen this image.

4. Allow the different images to form one image uniquely yours that symbolizes the quality of Dominion. Deepen and amplify this symbolic image.

(Continued on next page)

(Continued from previous page)

5. Slide this quality down through the right side of your body and place it on your right hip just above the pelvis. Breathe deeply as you sharpen the image symbolizing the quality of taking control, asserting yourself, or giving in the way you desire. Hold this image at your right hip point. Slowly move the image to the middle of your pelvis, directly below your naval. Breathe in and out of your pelvis area. As you affirm the quality of Dominion by stating, "I can take control and direct myself" continue deepening this image within you. Embrace the quality of control, perseverance, and endurance. See yourself emanating this quality from within yourself or other people.

6. After you finish meditating on the quality of Dominion, open your eyes and write down what you experience.

Putting Your Right Foot Forward

Cynthia became proficient at visualizing herself in her new roles and in taking action to get what she wanted. Exercising previously untapped power, she braved her new world step by step. She finished her advanced degree and certifications, bought a house, and assumed leadership roles. By listening carefully, evaluating, and taking a balanced position, she made an impact on other people. Mustering her courage, Cynthia challenged an authority figure in her workplace about an important issue and succeeded in changing his course of action.

The "girl" who once skirted the shadows, wanting only to receive the love she felt deprived of, transformed into a confident woman who commands attention, respect, and admiration. And she's enjoying every minute of it.

chapter eleven

The Face of Receptivity—*Hod*

The wise elder saw a man hurrying along the street, looking neither right nor left.

"Why are you rushing so?" he asked the man.

"I am after my livelihood."

"And how do you know," continued the elder, "that your livelihood is running on before you so that you have to rush after it? Perhaps it is behind you and all you need do to encounter it is to stand still—but you are running away from it!"

—IN POLSKY AND WOZNER, EVERYDAY MIRACLES, *EARLY MASTERS*

I can't change the direction of the wind, but I can adjust my sails to always reach my destination.

—JIMMY DEAN

It's all happening too fast! I've got to put on the brakes or I'll smack into something.

—MEL GIBSON

The best way to explain the Tree of Life's concept of Receptivity is in relationship to its giving counterpart, Dominion. We can measure our ability to receive (take in) in contrast to our ability to take action (give outwardly). The face of Receptivity monitors our thoughts and emotions pertaining to our activities. It is the ability to stand back and evaluate what you are doing and its effects on you and others.

Receiving relates to sensitivity. It enables you to clarify facts and tune into nuances so you can modify your actions according to your goals. Receptivity is knowing when to let go and allow something to happen, rather than pushing. It means yielding to a process, accepting the activity must follow its momentum before you can see where to use your energy.

Receptivity is connected to sincerity and gratitude as well. When your Receptivity is in balance, you genuinely appreciate the actions taking place in the world as well as the fruits of your labors. Acting with sincerity, you move earnestly, unencumbered by self-doubt and false intent, toward your goals.

As you act with Receptivity, you acknowledge the awe of co-creating that which you envision and you experience splendor.

Receptivity—letting go of control and accepting, or even asking for, what we need—can be frightening and difficult for many of us. However, when you are fully receptive, you are open to whatever happens. Of course, receptivity also requires governing what and how you receive into and give out from yourself. For example, if someone else's excessive giving actions overwhelm you, then you need to modify or stop the actions before they throw you off balance and erode your stability.

Biblical Archetype of Receptivity

The Old Testament gives the archetype of Receptivity to Aaron, the brother of Moses. As the high priest in charge of a temple, Aaron was responsible for creating a sacred space that inspired others to experience gratitude toward the Creator through their prayers and rituals.

Recalling the story of Moses, Aaron loyally assisted his brother in guiding the Israelites out of exile. Aaron followed Moses' lead, but they worked as a team. Aaron reportedly often communicated what Moses wanted to say, because Moses had a stuttering problem.

The primary lesson of the story of Aaron is that a receptive role is as important as a leadership role. To achieve balance in relationships we must balance activity with receptivity.

Aaron also had a weak side. He gossiped with Miriam against Moses. Although his receptivity enabled him to accompany Moses in doing G-d's work, it also, when imbalanced, allowed him to go along with the rebelling Israelites while Moses was on Mt. Sinai. This parable again illustrates that archetypes have balanced and imbalanced faces of the soul just as we do.

Exercise 25: How Does Your Face of Receptivity Appear?

The following statements depict a person whose face of Receptivity is in balance, monitoring actions, letting go, and allowing space. Place a checkmark next to each item that is more true than false about you.

1. I attend to details in my personal and professional life.
2. I take breaks from doing to receive the splendor of the world—to stop and smell the roses.
3. I assess the consequences of my actions.
4. I step back and go with the flow of a process emerging, rather than trying to control it.
5. I yield when it is appropriate to do so.
6. I easily adapt to change.
7. I have spiritual yearnings.
8. I graciously receive compliments and gifts from others.
9. I enjoy being hugged.
10. I delegate, trusting others to do their part.

The following statements exhibit imbalance in the quality of Receptivity. Check each statement that is more true than false about you.

1. I feel victimized and not able to act on what I need.
2. I act like a martyr, giving with disregard for my needs and goals.
3. I am passive.
4. I feel apathetic.
5. I am resigned.
6. I am dormant.
7. I acquiesce.
8. I feel lifeless.
9. I overestimate myself
10. I am extremely self-sacrificing.

Genesis of Receptivity

Receptivity (*Hod*) corresponds to the fifth day of Creation. The first creatures the Creator produced on the fifth day were fish—the first life-form with the ability to move where it wanted to go. The branch of Receptivity, in contrast to Dominion which can prevent free movement, provides us with the ability to change direction at will.

Cultivating Receptivity

Developing Receptivity is one of the core principles in the Tree of Life teachings. The Hebrew word Kabbalah comes from the root *le kebel*, which means "to receive." Receptivity provides access to all the faces of the Tree of Life. It opens you to the new ideas, information, images, sensations, events, relationships, and spiritual messages you need to take the steps in your life's journey. Have you ever, in hindsight, regretted missing an opportunity at work or in love after rejecting it too quickly?

To let in receptivity, you must let go of the belief that you must always be in control. You must re-examine your attitudes and let go of stubbornness, arrogance, and self-righteousness.

You can begin to cultivate receptivity by simply practicing your yielding and listening skills. Pay closer attention to what's going on around you. Listen to what people are actually saying and tune into the nuances of their expression, without projecting your thoughts into their messages. Consider new or neglected sources of information and inspiration. Be willing to practice restraint, tolerance, and stay quiet. You may find this difficult. Accepting something new can be hard. When traversing uncharted territory, people often become frightened and then put up their defenses. However, Receptivity is an essential ingredient to climbing the branches of your Tree of Life to harvest happiness, success, and health.

Giving on Her Terms

The Kabbalah notion of giving the beloved the symbol that is important to him or her reflects Receptivity on the level of action. Like many men, I dearly loved to buy clothes for my wife. However, I got carried away with that, caught up in my enjoyment in being expansive, and didn't at first notice she was displeased. In fact, she usually didn't like what I bought for her. Rather than providing a source of pleasure for both of us, as I had hoped, it sometimes turned into a point of contention later. When this happens, the giver feels hurt, and the receiver, believing the other's actions demonstrate he doesn't really know her, feels unloved. Realizing I needed to be more sensitive, I asked what I could give her that she would treasure as a symbol of my love for her. Her response was instantaneous: "Jewelry and perfume!" So now, we both enjoy it when I bring her gifts of perfume or jewelry from my travels abroad.

I'm Worth More than This

John, age 49, was an outgoing, successful middle-manager of a flourishing marketing firm. A competent supervisor, he very effectively helped others improve their productivity and efficiency. He generated and implemented creative ideas, and everyone apparently liked him. Yet, he became increasingly dismayed and depressed when other middle managers were promoted to higher ranks at higher salaries, while he remained in the same position.

He asked his co-workers why they thought he wasn't promoted, but their comments shed no light on his dilemma. What he didn't understand was that these people never gave him completely truthful responses. His drive and single-handed quests threatened both his peers and his superiors, who consequently didn't view him as a team player, an important element in business.

During a conversation with Joel, a close friend whom he had known for more than 20 years, he asked why Joel thought he wasn't moving up the corporate ladder. His friend hesitated anxiously and asked, "John, do you really want feedback?" Bewildered, John responded, "What do you mean, do I want feedback? Of course I do!" Joel chuckled and said, "Well, sometimes when you ask for advice, you seem to not really want to hear what I have to say." John assured his friend that this time he really did. Joel explained that, as one of John's best friends, he accepted and loved him just the way he was, but that some of his personality traits worked against him in the workplace. Joel went on, "If you want to get promoted, you must learn to listen to others, acknowledging their ideas, being less argumentative, and more willing to compromise and even to yield." (These were things John had a very difficult time doing!)

Joel was exactly right. John began to tune into others at work, asking their opinions, and seeking opportunities to work as part of team projects.

Transforming Toxicity

Ellen, age 35, was diagnosed with colon cancer. Many people who need to bolster their receptivity to love and support hold in bitter feelings and resentment, which eats them up inside, often resulting in physical problems in their lower bodies. Ellen was determined to cure herself. She had seen many traditional and alternative doctors. She suffered tremendous pain on her lower-right side.

Ellen was perpetual motion embodied. She never stopped. She held three jobs and worked every day, including weekends. Exploring the events and hurts of her life, it became clear she had maintained an exceedingly high activity level as far back as she could remember. An overachiever in virtually every outward aspect of her life, she had grown up always making perfect grades and behaving like a "good girl." Her family fostered her independence. However, she never learned how to give and take in intimate relationships. She secretly feared leaning on anyone. She was way over-balanced on the right side of her tree.

During one visualization, she focused on the pain in her gut and imaged memories of longing for her mother's unconditional love. She had always believed that the way to win her mother's love was through her achievements. Her pent-up anger burst out in sobs as she acknowledged she was tired of moving frenetically through her life. She mourned the many opportunities for love relationships she had passed up because she had not been receptive, clinging to her false belief that she needed no one. Her colon had been telling her that all along: she needed to give her right side a rest and develop her left face of Receptivity.

Ellen took better care of herself, working less, improving her diet, and doing things she enjoyed. She also accepted love and support from others. To her physician's amazement, her colon cancer went into remission!

Exercise 26: Cultivating the Face of Receptivity

1. Write the word Receptivity at the top of a sheet of paper. List the ways in which you need to better receive in your life. Remember, receiving means monitoring how much you give to yourself or others as well as allowing yourself to yield and step back. Can you recall a time when you were cautious before you said something? Perhaps it was when you met someone you liked or during a job interview. Perhaps it was listening, rather than giving advice, when a friend needed just to be heard. Receiving also means accepting and sometimes even asking for help from others. Can you remember allowing yourself to receive gladly and without reservation? Perhaps it was letting someone give you a warm hug, or giving yourself permission to take a break, or spilling your heart out to a friend.

2. Close your eyes and imagine the different parts of Receptivity one by one. Let the images and sensations flow through your mind and body. Continue to let memories of receptivity in your life surface.

3. Focus on what is happening within you. What are you experiencing? Fully experience the sensations arising in your body. Where in your body are the sensations occurring? Perhaps your friend's hug warmed your tummy. Perhaps you felt the tension evaporate from your body as you shared your worries with a confidante. Allow the different parts of receiving to form one image that uniquely symbolizes your face of Receptivity. Some people image a beautiful cup poised to receive or a peaceful lake. Others image getting a massage or submerging in a warm bath.

(Continued on next page)

(Continued from previous page)

4. Holding your symbol of Receptivity clearly in your imagination, move the image down through the left side of your body and hold it on your left hip. Breathe in and out of your left hip and deepen the image of Receptivity. Experience this quality radiating from the focal point of your left hip down through your left leg and left foot.

5. Slowly move this image into the middle of your upper pelvis, directly below your naval, and further deepen the image.

6. Deepen the image of Receptivity in the middle of your pelvis by affirming, "I am receptive to myself and others. I can monitor my actions. I act with sincerity." Embrace the quality of Receptivity. Visualize yourself emanating this quality outward first toward yourself or then toward other people.

7. After you finish meditating on the quality of Receptivity, open your eyes and write down what you experienced.

Less Can Be More

Jeff, the CEO and owner of his company, was ready to take action to be more open to himself and his needs and less giving toward others. He wanted to learn how to monitor his overzealous actions and to discern which boundaries to put on himself and others. He was ready to build a more stable dominion at work by strategically planning for the future.

To develop his qualities of Receptivity, Jeff focused on regulating actions. He spontaneously imaged this characteristic as a stopwatch. He felt he spent too much time on phone calls, which took him away from other important duties at his company. He successfully used the stopwatch image to develop restraint with phone conversations.

Setting Limits

Cynthia monitored her caretaking. She became more receptive to herself, and she knew and set her limits. With her romantic interests, she reflected on whether she was maintaining reciprocity between her giving to and receiving from the men she was dating. She experienced a major breakthrough when she adjusted her attitude from worrying whether she was pleasing others to considering whether they were pleasing her.

Learning to Lean

Michael learned to let go of needing to always control himself and everything in his environment. He opened up to receptivity by cultivating his willingness to accept assistance and his faith in others. That led him to tap into his right creative brain during imaging sessions, which produced powerful results, because he was now receptive to feeling emotions. Consequently, he opened up his heart and found his true calling.

chapter twelve

The Face of Stability—*Yesod*

When a man has to rise from one level to the next, prior to his ascent he must first undergo a descent. The paradox is the very purpose of the descent is the ascent . . . . Even when you fall in any way, you must never allow yourself to become off balance to the extent that you come to look down upon yourself or hold yourself in contempt. You should refuse to dwell on the matter even momentarily. Regardless of what happens to you in the end you will find that all your descents will be turned into great ascents and achievements because the purpose of descent is the ascent.

—NACHMAN OF BRESLOV
—*RESTORE MY SOUL*

The motto of life is "give and take." Everyone be both a giver and receiver. He who is not both is as a barren tree.

—MARTIN BUBER

It is not the strongest of the species that survive, nor the most intelligent, but the one most responsive to change.

—CHARLES DARWIN

The Trunk of Stability

The balance of giving and receiving in one's daily life produces what the Kabbalah and the Tree of Life teachings call Stability. The quality of Stability is found in the center of the lower trunk below the naval and in the pelvis area. This is the place where our legs connect with and support our hips, steadying us for walking on the ground. It is also the area on which martial artists primarily focus in their exercises to achieve stableness and balance. The quality of Stability, or equilibrium, derives from the lower tree trunk. People who exhibit Stability in their daily lives enjoy good health, professional success, and security within a close network of family and friends that often includes a spouse and children.

The movements from this area of the body during sexual intercourse are the natural rhythms between male and female energies that perpetuate the human species. The flow of giving and receiving during lovemaking, of taking charge and letting go, can be seen as the most creative act one can experience with the ultimate Creator. The sensitivity that a husband and wife share in expressing these energies can bring fulfillment to their conjugal/marital relationship.

A strong sense of security not only generates intimate relationships with one's spouse and resulting offspring, it also facilitates successful actions at work, in relationships, and in the community. Ultimately, when you achieve Stability and can maneuver smoothly between your Dominion and Receptivity, you probably will reap successes in most areas of your life.

Biblical Archetype of Stability

The archetype of Stability in the Bible is Joseph. In addition to his innumerable actions out in the world, Joseph expresses a wide range of emotions. The Kabbalists picked Joseph as the universal symbol of Stability because he always remained grounded and calm in his dealings with others. He experienced the worst of betrayals and pain when his brothers, jealous of him and his talents and his father's gift of a long coat of many colors, cast him into a pit and left him for dead. He did not panic when he was sold into slavery, but became a trusted servant. He stayed centered and did not betray his Egyptian master, when the master's wife tried to seduce him. When she falsely accused him and his master threw him into prison, he did not complain or feel martyred. He always made the best he could out of every disaster or challenge. He immediately took action and became a trusted overseer at the prison. He knew who he was and was ready when his opportunity came to interpret the dream of the Pharaoh.

When his brothers came to the Pharaoh begging for food for their people, the powerful Joseph did not take revenge. He did teach them a lesson and not tell them at first that he was the brother they had betrayed. But ultimately, he was kind to them and sent them home safely with food. Joseph was able to be in control, in charge of himself and others and be humble at the same time. He was a hero of balance, a man with a firm foundation who could weather all the tribulations and storms and come out on top.

Exercise 27: How Secure Is Your Center of Stability?

The following statements characterize a person who integrates giving and receiving energies resulting in Stability. If the majority of these statements apply to you, you are probably operating from a stable foundation and do not need to work on your face of Stability at this moment of your life.

Place a checkmark next to each statement that is more true than false about you.

1. I usually feel happy and optimistic about daily life and the future.
2. I am self-confident.
3. I have a reciprocal loving relationship with my partner/spouse/children.
4. I receive gratification from my work.
5. I am healthy.
6. I am sensitive to and mutually respective of other's needs and my own.
7. I feel secure about my future.
8. I feel equally comfortable leading and participating.
9. I delegate easily to others.
10. I can flow easily with change.

Cultivating Stability: Blending Dominion and Receptivity

By now the whole picture of how we achieve wholeness and stability is probably starting to gel for you. We truly empower ourselves only when we succeed in uniting our opposing energies into a single, focused power. We achieve Stability by simultaneously reigning and humbly serving in our worlds; by giving and receiving in equal measures; and by acting responsibly toward both others and ourselves. By trimming our overextended branches on the right and/or left sides of our trees until they're in balance with the stable center of our trunks: we will have achieved the middle path.

Blending the contrasting faces of your soul requires knowing that everything has its time and its place. Practically, that means learning to coordinate and to sometimes compromise conflicting desires within yourself and between you and others. You must be more willing and quick to both yield and stand your ground. Living a life of Stability, you're like a tree swaying gracefully in the winds of change, yet remaining firmly rooted at your foundation.

> For everything there is a season and a time for every matter under heaven:
> a time to be born, and a time to die;
> a time to plant, and a time to pluck up what is planted;
> a time to kill, and a time to heal;
> a time to break down, and a time to build up;
> a time to weep, and a time to laugh;
> a time to mourn, and a time to dance;
> a time to cast away stones, and a time to gather stones together;
> a time to embrace, and a time to refrain from embracing;
> a time to seek, and a time to lose;
> a time to keep, and a time to cast away;
> a time to rend, and a time to sew;
> a time to keep silence, and a time to speak;
> a time to love, and a time to hate;
> a time for war, and a time for peace.
> What gain has the worker from this toil?
>
> —ECCLESIASTES 3:1–8

The dynamics involved in cultivating Stability are akin to the dynamics of achieving balance in motion. For many years I was a full-time improvisational drummer. Music, just like humans, moves continuously through time and space. The drummer maintains the rhythm, the pulse, of the song, which requires being receptive to what the other musicians are playing. When a horn player accents a certain rhythm, the drummer accentuates his beat to complement the other musician's sounds, sharing that musical space together, then quickly moves back to center. To keep the music exciting and flowing, the drummer moves constantly between activity and receptivity while at the same time sustaining the main, or "bottom," pulse. We all can become the improvisational rhythm keepers of our daily lives, tuning in to the music within and around us. Knowing when to accent others and when to amplify ourselves. Knowing when to drop back and when to pick up the melody.

Loving with Limits

A father took his son to a toy store to shop for the boy's birthday. The father's best friend owned the store and invited the child to go through his store and pick out as many toys as he wanted within 15 minutes.

The father's initial reaction to his friend's gift was the desire to take dominion over his child and stop him to prevent him from taking too much! However, he curtailed his tendency to control and allowed his seven-year-old to tackle the opportunity himself. The boy soon grew very frustrated; overwhelmed with the freedom to pick absolutely anything, he couldn't concentrate or direct his actions. The father looked at the child with compassion and said, "I'm going to change the rules to help you out here. Why don't you choose two toys that you really, really want." Visibly relieved, the birthday boy quickly selected two special gifts.

This is a good example of creating stability in action in conjunction with the middle faces of compassion. The father demonstrated caring and respect for his son as well as the value of setting limits.

Stop the World I Want to Get Off!

Many of us feel overwhelmed with tending to all the details of our daily lives. Paul, age 29, worked long hours in a computer company. He was a highly productive employee who should have been making twice his salary. He was extremely loyal to his boss, who demanded a great deal from him. He pushed himself to meet deadlines and seldom allowed himself breathing room. He clearly turned over too much control to his work dominion.

His main complaint was that he didn't have sufficient time for his family or to develop his career. He needed to trim his branch of Dominion and expand his branch of Receptivity. Because he was a detail-oriented person by nature, he made a detailed schedule that included absolute time-out from work. He periodically took off half days from work, which he used to create his resume and career development activities. He asked people outside the company for help in finding new job opportunities.

Many people never realize that failing to step back and monitor their actions prohibits them from ever giving themselves space to grow. Because Paul worked on commission, he always feared that if he took off time, he would lose income and upset his personal finances. In granting himself time out from his over-activity (Dominion) to bolster his Receptivity while taking refuge in his face of faith (roots of reverence), he let go of his insecurity about money, trusting he would make new business inroads.

One of Paul's main challenges was his reluctance to lean on others for help. Like many of us, he mistakenly equated being open and vulnerable with being "weak." He used the Tree of Life principles to strengthen his ability to network, to receive feedback and assistance from others, which actually expanded his domain.

To his surprise, when he gave himself space and shared his needs with others, especially his enthusiasm for challenging work, he connected with Stephen, a wealthy entrepreneur who took an active interest in him. Paul was shocked when Stephen offered him a partnership in his venture. He had never considered the possibility of someone in power wanting to partner with him. The notion ran counter to his old patterns of blind loyalty that had pinned him to a stagnant position with an unstable company. Within a year, Paul was CEO of an innovative Internet start-up that has since taken off.

His new pattern of letting go of control also positively affected his marriage. He opened up emotionally to and asked for more help from his wife, who, in return, felt closer to him. He achieved greater balance in giving of himself and receiving from others in both his personal and professional relationships. He marveled in the happy paradox that, in becoming more receptive and vulnerable to others, he had become a leader.

It Takes Two to Tango

My wife had always wanted me to take ballroom dance lessons with her. Like many men, I resisted the idea. She kept nudging me, repeatedly showing me different ads in the newspaper. I would always say the lessons cost too much. But she was tenacious and came up with discounted tango lessons. When I learned one of my friends had taken ballroom dance lessons with his wife, it motivated me to give it a whirl. One of the first dances we learned was the tango. I especially appreciated it when the teacher would say, "Ladies, follow the lead of your man." I told myself, I am coming to take tango lessons forever! This would be even better than going to marital therapy! In the process of cultivating something in me that she desired, my wife had to cultivate something within herself. If she wanted me to master tango, she needed to learn to follow! Of course, in actuality, good ballroom dancing requires that both people be in tune with one another and move gracefully in the same direction. They perform this unified dance from opposing sides, with one partner moving forward while the other moves backward, or one moving to the left as the other moves to the right. I can't say we actually achieved this state of grace in our ballroom dancing, but it provides a good analogy of balance in motion—and thinking about it always makes me laugh.

Managing Pain Before It Manages You

Iris, age 42, suffered a great deal from chronic back pain resulting from two car accidents within one year. Because she prided herself on nourishing others and her fierce independence, her disabling pain humbled her considerably. Convinced her successful and rewarding career as a marketing salesperson was over, she grew increasingly despondent. Iris discovered that her resistance to accepting help from others contributed greatly to her difficulties. She needed to learn to balance herself by leaning on her husband as well as on friends and colleagues to do things for her. To her surprise, others were more than receptive! Yielding to the assistance of others enabled her to take control of some activities, albeit initially in bite-size proportions. She stopped pushing herself when she needed to rest and relax, and she let others help. As she did that, her back pain lessened proportionately.

Stabilizing Your Trunk of Security

Now let's help you strengthen your face of Stability by focusing on balancing the bottom triad of the lower faces of your Tree of Life. On the right side of the tree we give out assertively in the realm of Dominion. On the left side of the tree we allow ourselves to receive with Receptivity. Then we meet in the middle-lower trunk fulcrum to blend these qualities into a balanced foundation.

As with the upper and middle triads, the following meditations focus on each of these qualities individually until they are clear in our minds. Then we image them and bring them together. Remember, to act from a position of stability, we must develop both the right- and left-lower sides before we can blend them into a harmonious foundation.

Exercise 28: Creating Stability

1. Close your eyes and focus on your breathing. Bring back the image that symbolizes your forces of Dominion. Remember, dominion means taking control and initiating in the world, not controlling everything. See yourself directing yourself the way you choose.

2. Once you have clearly retrieved your vision of Dominion, bring this image down to the focal point of your lower-right branch, your right hip. Gently hold the image of Dominion to your right hip point, deepening the image and letting it permeate that area.

3. As you continue breathing deeply to sharpen this image of Dominion, let it emanate out from your right hip through your right leg and foot. Experience the sensations occurring in that region of your body. Visualize yourself putting forward your right foot to move toward any task you set your mind to. Envision yourself as goal-oriented. Still holding the image of Dominion at your right hip point, call up your image of Receptivity. Deepen the image of Receptivity with your steady breathing and experience the quality of Receptivity within yourself. Remember, receptivity is the ability to stand back and monitor that which you are initiating or giving. It means giving to others and yourself with sincerity and balance, knowing when to yield and when to step forward.

4. Once you have this image of Receptivity fixed in your upper branches, slowly move it down to your left hip and hold it there. Inhale and exhale evenly to deepen this quality in your left hip point.

(Continued on next page)

(Continued from previous page)

5. Now, let the image of Receptivity emanate from your left hip point down through your left leg and foot. Experience the sensations occurring in the lower-left region of your body. Envision yourself mastering the quality of Receptivity, able to step back from your activity to receive sincerely from others and yourself.

6. Focus simultaneously on the images of Dominion on your right-hip point and Receptivity on your left-hip point, until the two images are equally sharp and in perfect balance.

7. Bring together these two images into the middle of your upper pelvis, until they fuse into a single form. Synthesize the blended image into a new, distinctive image of Stability. Let this image appear spontaneously.

8. Hold the image of Stability in your upper-middle pelvic area, breathing evenly to deepen the image, blending the qualities of initiating and receiving. Activate the quality of Stability, envisioning it manifested in your actions. Experience the sensations occurring in your upper-middle pelvis.

9. Affirm this quality within yourself by saying, "I am stable. I have a firm foundation in my life. I can give and receive simultaneously. I can both stand back to gauge my activities as well as initiate action to create success in my relationships, and in my personal, professional, and spiritual pursuits."

10. Continue to experience and embrace the quality of Stability within you, focusing on your breathing. When you are ready, slowly open your eyes. If you want to, write down what you experienced, particularly the images you received from this exercise.

Why Humans Were Created
On the sixth day, G-d created man. Man's purpose was to maintain Dominion over the earth while serving as the Receptivity center to the Creator. The Creator produced humans to give the unmanifested Endless Light arms and legs with which to do His work in its garden.

Balance in Motion

Cynthia acknowledged her pattern of over-giving to her husbands, smothering them with excessive care-taking and attention, then doing an about-face and distancing herself when she felt her love was not reciprocated. By honing her monitoring skills, she had learned to recognize when she was about to overstep her giving boundaries. She also had stopped letting others take advantage of her. Committed to paying greater attention to her giving and receiving processes, she was ready to take action to balance Dominion with Receptivity and strengthen her Stability. As a result, she gained more of what she wanted and needed, which increased her self-confidence, which, in turn, inspired her to take more action in her domain and to expand into other arenas.

Jeff, with all his conscious work and study, had succeeded in balancing the Receptivity and Dominion faces of his tree. He became more receptive to listening to his body, tending to his needs, and delegating to others. These receptive steps gave him more time for himself and his family, which consequently improved his health and relaxed his attitude toward work, which led to positive monitored action. His right- and left-lower qualities and actions aligned to bring him greater Stability in all areas of his life.

Have you ever watched a professional surfer ride a wave? At times, he (or she) deliberately moves to the right, at times to the left, to keep himself on top of the water. Sometimes the balancing motions of his body are radical, leaning far to the left, then far to the right at seemingly impossible angles. But as he achieves greater stability on the crest of the wave, his motions become more subtle, but equally important. That's balance in motion personified.

Creating stability in our lives involves learning how to ride the wave and developing the sensitivity to know precisely when and in which direction to lean to secure our balance. Only then can we reach the shore, where our goals await us.

part six

balancing
your faces

Introduction

This part of the book has two chapters. Chapter 13, "Drawing Wisdom from Your Ancestral Rings," is a resource to use when you're having difficulty developing one or more of the faces of your tree. Like many people, you may be unable to immediately embrace the balanced qualities of all the faces of your soul. You may need to do some extra work on healing wounds from your past that may be interfering with developing balance in your life. To fully develop your whole tree, you must work with the generations from within to help heal the imbalances that have existed in your family.

Chapter 14 will help you put together the teachings of all the triads. Michael, Cynthia, and Jeff, who have been sharing their stories throughout this book, will summarize their Tree of Life journeys through charts. Their examples will give you an opportunity to reflect on where you are on the various branches of your tree of life map. This chapter also includes blank charts for you to use in assessing your individual faces on the branches of your Tree of Life.

chapter thirteen

Drawing Wisdom from Your Ancestral Rings

> I keep in mind the sins (actions) of the fathers for their descendants, to the third and fourth (generations). But for those who love Me and keep my commandments, I shall love for thousands (of generations).

> —"Yithro in Exodus," *The Living Torah*

The Tree of Life rebalancing process works completely only when we've healed our ancestral wounds. The rings of the tree's trunk contain the wisdom of the generations. The Disney movie, *Pocahontas,* includes a beautiful modern example of this metaphor. Whenever Pocahontas, a young American Indian woman, feels confused, she consults an old willow tree. As she sits before the tree, the trunk opens up into an image of a wise old grandmother's face with compassionate eyes and kind smile. The elder spirit talks gently and directly to Pocahontas, helping her resolve some of the dilemmas she faces in her life.

Similarly, the voices of our ancestors call out from the depths of the rings found in the trunk and torso of our bodies. These sages of our collective past want us to tap into their wisdom to help guide us in living life more fully.

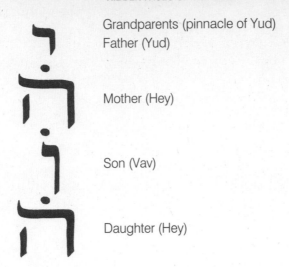

Grandparents (pinnacle of Yud)
Father (Yud)

Mother (Hey)

Son (Vav)

Daughter (Hey)

The Tetragrammaton of the Tree of Life teachings, the four sacred letters found within the Kabbalah, contain the wisdom of the generations.

As discussed in chapter 3, "The Face of Faith," these four letters can be written vertically or horizontally. From top to bottom the letters are Yud, Hey, Vav, and Hey. If you look closely at the top of the Yud, you will see a point at the pinnacle. This represents the place where we can hear our grandparents' voices. It is only a dot, because their voices are far in the past. The Kabbalists refer to this distant point as "Ancient of Days." From this upper-most point in the natural world, we can tap into the unitive center of will through the wisdom of our grandparents.

The curvature of the Yud represents the wisdom contained within our fathers (*Abah*). The top Hey is associated with the wisdom of our mothers (*Imah*).

The lower two letters are considered the third generation, with the Vav denoting the parents' son (*Arik Anpin*) and the bottom Hey their daughter (*Nukka*). Another way of looking at the Vav and bottom Hey is as male active and female receptive energies found within all of us. The Kabbalah refers to these images as *Partzufim*, the "faces, or archetypes, of the Creator."

Although, in reality, many of our descendants were/are not well balanced, the generations found within the Tree of Life's trunk symbolize the balanced, wise aspects of our grandparents, parents, and selves. Reconnecting with our respective Tree of Life families helps us restore balance and gain wisdom from deep within the trunk of our bodies.

Regenerating Our Roots

If you walk through the forest, you will see trees that are older than others. You will find healthy trees and sickly trees, thriving trees and straggly trees. You will see trees that are off balance and leaning to one side. You will also find trees with broken branches and crowded trees with no room to grow.

Similarly, the rings inside our trunks, reflecting the generations that came before us, often have not received sufficient sunlight, nutrients, and soil to grow properly. Some of our ancestors transplanted themselves in other lands, often losing contact with their original roots. This is particularly true for those of us in the United States whose family forests are indigenous to Europe or other places in the world. The deeply embedded pain of ancestors who were uprooted against their will or wishes and forced out of their homelands passes on to future generations.

We carry around inside us our ancestry (great-grandparents, grandparents, parents, even our earlier selves), often unaware of how their eternal presence affect our daily lives. To re-establish a connection with the "good" part, the wisdom, of our ancestral rings, we must heal the wounds of our ancestral family. I call this "healing our intragenerational family." It is the most powerful and heart-rending work we can do to free ourselves from deeply embedded suffering.

Many people struggle to embrace the different qualities on the Tree of Life because they are unhealthy at the very center of their trunks, where intense ancestral pain has festered. When that is the case, we must undergo a cleansing process to regenerate the root systems of our inner generations.

Accessing the wounds that one generation passes on to the next enables us to reveal and embrace our deepest fears, yearnings, hurts, hopes, and dreams. We can trace these patterns in our individual family trees through our parents and grandparents, bonding to our ancestors in ways we thought were impossible. We experience a profound understanding of our wounds as they are connected to the chains of time, to our histories. When we choose to engage in healing these wounds, we release our ancestors and ourselves from the fetters of long perpetuated, deeply embedded patterns of suffering.

Michael always had difficulty allowing himself to love. As you know from the earlier accounts in this book, after leaving the protective environment of his military career, he worried about creating new career pathways. He felt he could never lean on anyone or share his vulnerabilities. These patterns had deeply wounded him. Michael came from a long string of military men who never allowed themselves to feel or appear "weak." He, like his father and grandfather before him, felt lonely inside but would never admit it. Michael carried the battle scars of the ancestral male warriors he tried to emulate.

Cynthia "inherited" her ancestral pain from her mother. Her mother was sick off and on throughout Cynthia's childhood, and she often served as her mother's caretaker when her father was away on duty. She died when Cynthia was 14 years old, leaving her feeling unloved and abandoned.

The Inner Family

All human beings experience periods of emotional imbalance at some time in their lives. At various points in our childhood, we all feel vulnerable. As we grow up, we accumulate internal images of others and ourselves through constant interactions with our environment. Early in our development, we derive most of these images from our experiences with our parents, siblings, and grandparents. All these early interactions comprise our internal family system. The different parts of ourselves result, in large part, from behaviors we learned to satisfy the demands and expectations of parents or other influential people in our daily lives. Over time, these external expectations can lead us to identify with what others project on us. Parents often project their imbalances onto their children, thus perpetuating the sufferings of one generation to another.

Michael learned his dead father and grandfather were still very much alive inside him. When he started to work at imaging his inner family, he understood the pain he was experiencing was an extension of the wounds of his father and grandfather. He realized how critical and domineering his paternal grandfather had been toward his father and that his father felt compelled to maintain absolute control to "be a man." He then understood the source of his father's anger and that his father's anger had transferred to him. Michael very much wanted to break this intragenerational legacy.

Cynthia's inner family was suffering. Children who become caretakers of their parents become old before their time. Her mother's illness and early death had prevented her from providing Cynthia with the support she had always wanted to give her daughter. Cynthia's mother also felt abandoned by her husband, who never understood the impact of her illness. Consequently, she had been overly dependent and demanding of Cynthia. Cynthia discovered within herself a wise—but also very lonely, needy, and insecure—child who felt unloved and was overly responsible and felt obligated to nurture the adults around her.

Our Imbalanced Branches

The branches of the Tree of Life represent the divine manifestations of the highest power of the universe, G-d. Each of these qualities reflects the healthy and "good" aspects of the human spirit. However, these aspects can become imbalanced within us, diminishing our health and our good work in the world. As we have seen in previous chapters, for example, excess Dominion can overcontrol or overwhelm us, and extreme Receptivity can martyr us or drown us in negativity. Loving without boundaries can cause us to become smothering or overly dependent on others. Conversely, too many rigid boundaries can produce stubbornness, faultfinding, and rigidity, which won't let love in.

These imbalances form a variety of internal patterns that can distance us from our inner wisdom. A person's inner genealogy might include, for example, a controlling father, a victimized mother, and a stubborn child. Perhaps the ancestral map instead comprises a martyred father, a judgmental mother, and a protective child who defends the passive father against the demanding mother. Another person's internal family tree might consist of a passive father, a hopeless mother, and a dejected child. Attaching ourselves to these imbalances inhibits us from cultivating the essence of our sacred branches on our Trees of Life. To fully actualize the balanced purity of all the faces of our souls, we must heal the imbalanced interactions within our internal lineage.

When Michael explored his inner family further, he realized not only did he carry his father's and grandfather's over-Dominioned pain, he also carried the wounds of his mother's unhappiness with her marriage. His mother was a dutiful wife who placated his father. She was terrified of him and felt and behaved more like a little girl than a woman. Michael dug deep into the familial history inside him and resurfaced childhood emotions of feeling depressed and victimized by his father. He revisited his feelings of helplessness to protect his mother and of abandonment at her inability to protect him. The imbalanced branches of his parents and of his child self continued into his adult life. He recognized that he was repeating parts of his family drama with his wife and children and needed to change these patterns to become whole. To restore balance to his inner tree and allow it to flourish, he had to regenerate his roots.

Cynthia's Tree of Life map revealed to her that her inner faces were out of balance. The face of her mother was smothering. Although Cynthia's mother loved her, she let her over-dependence on her daughter override that love. Her father, unreceptive to understanding either her mother's or Cynthia's needs, had allowed his face of strength to turn to harsh judgment and emotional remoteness. As a result, Cynthia had overextended her branch of love and neglected her branch of strength. She did not possess a strong sense of self and had difficulty setting clear boundaries. These childhood patterns had persisted throughout her adulthood.

Glowing Faces

At its core, even the most imbalanced of our faces contains positive attributes. Only by staying off balance for a long time do the negative attributes of our faces emerge. Our challenge is to peel back the emotional husks that block the positive qualities of each face within us, liberating their inherent glow of light

We can shed these husks to reveal our inner glow by acknowledging, expressing, and then letting go of our ancestral pain. The seeker of spiritual balance must "express his yearning and longing in words," as the great Kabbalist Nachman of Breslov said. The Tree of Life teachings encourage you to speak your pain out loud with fervor—as if the Highest Power in the universe were listening. It is through this expressing of your full range of emotions that you release the sufferings of your internal lineage and align with the balanced archetypes within you, (*Partzufim*). Your aggrieved inner family's unspoken words become your spoken words, their unexpressed emotions your expressed emotions, and their imbalanced faces your balanced faces.

This renewal process involves reconciling all members of our intragenerational family—healing the ancestral wounds of our inner selves, parents, grandparents. and great-grandparents.

Creating Unity within the Inner Family

Unification lies at the heart of any spiritual work that focuses on self-healing. The goal of working on your inner family is to reunite the disconnected family images within you. This process consists of four main stages.

1. Recognition. Discerning the different parts of your inner family that need to work better together.

Michael reached the first stage of recognition when he developed greater understanding of his pain stemming from his inner family of mother, father, and self. He successfully identified and assessed the imbalanced faces of his mother's passivity, his father's overbearingness, and his face of fearfulness and despair.

Cynthia discovered that her relationship difficulties with men came from sabotaging herself by taking on a caretaking role with them as she had with her mother. She realized the frightened child inside, the result of her mother's early death and her father's unavailability, continued to fear abandonment and accordingly to overextend herself appeasing others.

2. Acceptance. Embracing the different aspects of your internal family, allowing each to express their individual needs openly and honestly.

Through imagery Michael reconnected the images of his father and mother. He expressed for the first time his pent-up fear toward his father and disappointment at his mother's failure to protect him in the way he needed. He wept for the child within who felt so vulnerable and mistreated. He finally accepted his deeply embedded inner family pain.

Cynthia allowed her mother's voice to express her grief about her illness and longing to take better care of her daughter. The child within Cynthia expressed her frustration with never being allowed to be a child and revealed her litany of unmet needs. She even removed her stoic father's mask of fortitude and expressed his fear and grief in not providing a stable family for his daughter, wife, and himself.

3. Coordination. Engaging all parts of our inner family in a dialog, exploring the central need of each from the others.

Michael continued to have inner conversations with his parents. However, the transformation occurred when he was able to step into his father's shoes. Through Michael's voice, the spirit of his father expressed how lonely he was and that he hadn't wanted to be "strong" but hadn't known any other way. Weeping, he said he loved Michael and was sorry he had not been more affectionate and accessible. Michael healed the wounds of his father he had carried around and let them go. He also let his mother talk with her husband and her son. In Michael's imagery, she communicated how angry she was with her husband for being self-centered, impatient, and angry. She acknowledged how difficult his father's sternness and her passivity had been for Michael and that her inability to relieve her son's pain depressed her. She said she felt helpless to change her interactions with his father. She expressed anger at Michael's father for not being a more loving husband and more patient parent. Michael wept with relief at allowing all members of his inner family to speak openly and honestly about their feelings. He further liberated himself by expressing to his father his need to be held, nurtured, and appreciated for his good traits.

In Cynthia's imagination, she let her child self speak with her internal father image. She told him he never listened, ignored her needs, and was overly critical. Then she let herself experience the gentle parts of her father's spirit she had forgotten, for example, when he held her and talked softly with her. She told him how much she appreciated these special moments. She also imaged her mother expressing her profound love for her. In her real life growing up with her parents, these types of honest interchanges never took place. Creating this open, loving dialog with her inner family was healing for her.

4. Coherence. Establishing a unifying foundation of understanding and forgiveness, based the mutual respect for the individual needs of all members of your inner family

Through coordinating his inner family, Michael could picture the family they could have been, listening to each other's needs and compassionately resolving conflicts. As his inner family conversed, the sharp edges of pain within him softened and he felt more whole. He achieved a new level of understanding that enabled him to discharge much of his pain, leaving him with a sense of unity and renewed balance. What's more, this process mobilized him to trust others, to share his real self, and to ask for help in finding the work he wanted.

As Cynthia absolved the emotional burdens of her inner family that she had carried for so long, a tremendous weight lifted from her soul. Letting her inner father, mother, and child speak their piece, and make their peace—and embracing the positive interactions along with the negative—gave her stability and a greater sense of self.

Exercise 29: Healing Your Inner Family Archetype

One of the best ways to tap into imbalances with our inner ancestors is through meditation and guided imagery, such as those introduced in previous chapters. Imagery gives us direct access to both positive attributes and painful wounds that emerge during the healing process.

This exercise will help you identify imbalances within your inner family to which you can direct your healing work.

NOTE: It is best to have someone guide you through the meditation. You can also record the directions on audio tape or disk and play it back when you are ready to meditate.

1. Close your eyes and breathe evenly, focusing your attention on inhaling and exhaling through your nose. Allow a spontaneous image of your family of origin to emerge in your mind's eye, envisioning yourself in the place you consider your childhood home. Where in the house is each person located? What are they doing? Are any family members speaking to each other? Who is closest to whom? Is anybody isolating or being excluded? What kind of atmosphere permeates the household? How do the people interact with each other? Is anyone in conflict with anyone else? How are they dealing with this conflict? Who is experiencing the greatest pain? Who most needs love in this family? Focus on that person.
2. Move closer to the person in the most pain. What is his or her facial expression and body posture? What is the source of this person's pain? What do they want most from the others and for himself or herself? Open up to this pain. See it, feel it, hear it, experience it, giving your inner family the gift of healing awareness.

(Continued on next page)

(Continued from previous page)

3. Once you grasp the nature and depth of this grievously wounded person's pain, step back from this inner family member and take three cleansing breaths. When you're ready to continue, invite your inner familial images to speak with each other. (You can silently image this conversation or vocalize it, whichever is most comfortable for you.) Encourage your inner family members, including yourself, to express their emotions and needs honestly and fully. Let them speak their minds and from their hearts. Allow the feelings to flow freely through you; experience them completely without inhibition. If you feel like crying or expressing your anger, let these feelings out. Take notice of the sensations you are experiencing (i.e., tingling, heat, nausea, burning, tension) and direct your speech from these pleasant or unpleasant sensations.

4. When the conversation ends, after all your inner family members have said what they needed to say to the others, open your eyes. If you'd like, write down what you experienced.

Healing Our Ancestral Wounds

Healing and uniting our inner ancestors next involves reconnecting with our grandparents and sometimes our great-grandparents. As you go through this process, you will experience the following 5 stages of healing: discovering, expressing, empathizing, loving, and forgiving.

1. *Discovering.* Becoming aware of deeply embedded ancestral *pain* that has manifested *mentally*, *emotionally*, or *physically* in your life.

Michael realized he needed to also release his father's pain around his relationship with his father, Michael's grandfather. Only by imaging his father's relationship with his grandfather, by opening and transforming these intragenerational wounds of his inner family, could Michael heal the imbalances in himself.

To her surprise, Cynthia's work also involved revisiting inner wounds that streched back to her grandparents. Her maternal grandmother had died when Cynthia's mother was a teenager, just as Cynthia's mother had died when Cynthia was a teenager. Cynthia's mother, like Cynthia, also had assumed the role of her ailing mother's caretaker, with no one to tend to her needs. Throughout her adult life, Cynthia had pondered this mysterious pattern in her family.

2. *Expressing*. Verbalizing your inner family's fear, sadness, or anger over the manifestations of intragenerational wounds. This may encompass losses you have suffered as a result of feelings of abandonment, insecurity, or deprivation passed along to you from earlier generations. If you feel an abundance of grief, you may need to express anger to release the pain and move on.

Michael's inner father expressed his anger at Michael's inner grandfather for putting excessive pressure on him to be perfect. He vented his frustration at feeling unable to ever let down his guard and just have fun, at being inhibited by his constant fear of doing or saying something wrong. His inner father wept, feeling the loss of having no emotional connection with his own father.

While Cynthia was growing up, she often heard stories about how her mother and grandmother never got along. They either argued incessantly or refused to speak with one another for long periods of time. In her intragenerational imaging, Cynthia's inner mother talked to her inner grandmother about the fear and sadness she felt about her illness and impending death. As she allowed the spirits of her inner mother and grandmother to converse within her,

Cynthia experienced a sensation of releasing the dead to go to their rests, which gave her inner peace.

3. *Empathizing*. Feeling compassion for the pain of your inner family members. This stage is at the center of the healing process. When you can "walk in the other's shoes," you can often appreciate and connect with the other's suffering. Experiencing sorrow for the other can, in turn, evoke many other powerful emotions within you, such as remorse for alienating yourself from that person. This empathetic grief typically generates tears of caring.

Michael wept for both his inner father's losses as well as for his own. He expressed regret and sorrow for the many years that had gone by without making a positive connection with his father. He felt both his own and his inner father's grief, longing for a father who loved him and whom he could love.

Cynthia became aware of the loneliness felt by all the members of her inner family. She appreciated the tragic imbalances that had been carried down through the generations. During one session, she envisioned all three generations of women, including herself, as emotional orphans who had no stable, nurturing homes and deeply wept.

Gates of Tears

The Zohar *(Book of Splendor)*, an early Kabbalistic text contains the following passage describing the process of feeling sorrow and its connection to the highest spirituality.

> The answer is that from the day of the destruction of the temple, all gates to Heaven have been closed, but the Gates of Tears have not been closed, and suffering and sadness are expressed in tears. Standing over the Gates of Tears are certainly heavenly beings, and they break down the bars and locks of iron and allow the tears to enter so the entreaties of the grieving supplicants go through and reach the Holy King, and the place of Divine Presence is grieved by the sorrow of him who prays, as it stands

(Continued on next page)

(Continued from previous page)

written, "In all their afflictions, He is afflicted . . . ": (Isaiah 63:9 Old Testament, the Bible).

Through weeping, you can discover a great deal about yourself, others, and spirituality, which aides in healing. An early Kabbalist discusses the healing property of tears and refers to the first volume of the Zolar when he confesses:

> By much weeping, like a well, and suffering, I became more able to be transformed into a flowing stream, a fountain of wisdom: No secret was revealed to me, nor wondrous apprehension, but afterwards I became like dust and wept before the Creator of the Universe like a spring, lest I should be rejected from the light of this face, and for the sake of getting apprehensions out of the source of wisdom, and I became as a flowing well weeping." In *Idell, Moishe Kabbalah, New Perspectives,* page 86.

Experiencing sorrow opens oneself up to deepening compassion, which softens the heart. This process generates mutual empathy between family members' accumulated ancestral wounds. This, in turn, strengthens and expands your middle trunk, where your balanced qualities reside. This is the apex of a deep, spiritual connection.

When Michael experienced his father's pain toward his grandfather, he wept as much as he had when he worked on his own pain toward his father. These heartfelt tears washed away his protective shell, making him feel softer and more open, and renewed him with powerful energy. He felt compassion for his father. He imaged expressing to his dead father that he understood his pain and was sorry for the losses in his life and for what he had gone through with his father.

Cynthia, through weeping for the first time over her intragenerational losses, allowed herself to open in ways she had never before experienced. She felt a growing strength of the heart and a determination to change her family legacy. She felt tremendous compassion toward her mother, grandmother, and herself for all of the suffering each had endured from their shared experiences with illness and death.

4. *Loving*. Accepting all members of your ancestral tree with a profound bond of caring and acceptance. When you feel compassion and express love for your inner family, you extend your branches and stabilize the trunk of your Tree of Life. You experience a lifting of your spirit, a resurgence of energy, and a reconnection with your roots.

Michael spontaneously expressed love for his father during a very moving imaged conversation. He shared with his father all the things he admired about him, including his strength, perseverance, and ability to take responsibility. He forged a new healing, and liberating, bond with his father.

Cynthia replaced her anger at feeling abandoned with feelings of love and connectedness toward her mother and grandmother. She also experienced the unexpressed love she had always known they felt for her but had never allowed herself to receive.

5. *Forgiving*. Releasing the pain of and blame for our ancestral wounds. Forgiveness progresses naturally from compassionate love to finally ease the suffering of buried or persistent past losses. Letting go of expectations of your loved ones often yields forgiveness.

Michael forgave his father and released his expectations of him that had created pressure inside Michael for a long time. He released some of his pent-up anger that he had been unable to deal with previously. He felt greatly relieved at finally letting go and accepting his father with greater understanding, compassion, love, and forgiveness.

Cynthia realized she had been holding many grudges against her mother as well as her father for not protecting and nurturing her. She understood her father had allowed his grief to distance him from the family. She let go of her expectations of others. She also built on her growing strength in blending her abilities to give and receive love and to develop her career. Some people undermine their spiritual growth by holding on to childhood resentments and by not realizing their futures are in their hands. By letting go of the pain of her past, Cynthia moved forward in her journey toward a more balanced life.

As you continue this process of inner family healing, the roots regenerate and the inner trunk expands further. The Kabbalah associates this energy as the blending of all the balanced qualities that are the hidden faces of your soul contained in the highest branch of Keter (the crown on top of the tree). These qualities are unity, understanding, wisdom, love, strength, compassion, dominion, receptivity, stability, and faith. These qualities when unified will bring deep peace and joy!

Once you've healed the intragenerations of your family tree, you can fully realize the unity of all the attributes of your Tree of Life. If you get stuck along the way, you can use meditation and imaging to help free yourself and continue your journey toward refining these qualities.

NOTE: Portions of this chapter have been excerpted, with changes, from *Transforming the Inner and Outer Family: Humanistic and Spiritual Approaches to Mind–Body Systems Therapy,(1995)* by Dr. Sheldon Z. Kramer, Haworth Press.

Exercise 30: Unifying the Family Archetypes and Realigning Your Branches

This exercise is a follow-up to Exercise 29, "Healing Your Inner Family Archetype." In that exercise you worked on the different parts of your family tree. This meditation works well when you get stuck on one of the faces of your Tree of Life you want to embrace. For example, you can use this exercise to deepen a healing connection between the generations within you.

1. Close your eyes. Take in a deep breath quickly through your nose. Hold it, then let it out slowly through your mouth. Continue breathing evenly in this manner as you focus on the quality of the Tree of Life branch you need to cultivate. Say this word out loud (for example, Love).

2. Allow a spontaneous image of your family (including you) to appear. Envision your mother and/or father as children. See your grandparents, parents, brothers, and sisters. Does your mother or father need to express anything to their parents about this quality in your life? Perhaps they still have pain they need to discuss with their parents or siblings.

3. Invite the family images to speak to each other and listen to what they say. (You can either speak these words out loud or through your internal voice.) Experience the energy and emotions as your different family archetypes converse, expressing their needs and hurts. Feel any anger expressed by your parents or their siblings. Let your grandparents or uncles or aunts talk back. Let the images take turns talking. Is there anything else you need to say to your parents or your brothers and sisters? Let everyone talk from their heart.

(Continued on next page)

(Continued from previous page)

4. Imagine a white glowing light above your head: the light of *Keter*—your unitive center of will. Slowly draw the light down through the crown of your head and your upper branches, immersing yourself and your family in soothing light.

5. Experience the regenerating of your roots, the realigning of your branches, and the expansion of your trunk as these family images heal in your heart. Feel restorative balance spread to all the branches of your Tree of Life, especially those you most need to cultivate.

We sometimes can clearly envision where we want to go and what we want to do, but can't seem to act on those visions because we're blocked by inner family past wounds. Cynthia and Michael worked a great deal with these exercises to heal their childhood pains, which released deeply embedded fears and allowed them to forgive their families. It softened their defenses and freed them to act courageously upon their visions. You, too, can utilize these meditations to work on removing the intragenerational wounds that may be interfering with your progress in cultivating specific branches of your Tree of Life.

If you are unable to embrace the quality of a particular branch after completing the meditations you've learned so far in this book, or if these exercises produced too much inner turmoil for you, stop using them. You may need to do more intensive work and consult with a mental health professional or counselor who can help you work through any inner pain you're holding.

chapter fourteen

Integrating All Your Faces
of Your Tree of Life

Charting Your Tree of Life Progress

Now that you've looked at your indiv idual faces and learned how
all the branches interrelate, you are ready to chart your whole personality on your Tree of Life map. This will help you determine
where you are on your journey and what you must do to generate
growth. You may need to go back to the various assessment exercises and bring them together into a complete picture.

This simple and painless self-assessment is comprised of two
parts. First, you'll chart the current state of each branch on your
Tree of Life. Then you'll chart what you need to do to cultivate any
qualities that are out of balance. Both charts are designed to help
you assess your mind, emotions, and actions for the ten individual
faces of your soul. Faith is not charted because it has no contracting
and expanding qualities. As you align the other triads and get positive results in your life, faith and confidence will also appear.

Chart I, "My Tree of Life: How My Life Looks Now," is a tool
for evaluating where you stand in your spiritual development at this
moment. Be honest with yourself about where you sense and know
you are out of balance. Be gentle with yourself and smile at yourself, if you can. We're all human.

Chart 2, "My Tree of Life: What I Need for Balance," serves as a guide to the future you envision for yourself, once you've rectified the imbalances revealed on Chart 1. This second chart lets you plan your goals and map the paths you must take to achieve them. When working on your second chart, remember that a hallmark of the Tree of Life journey is blending opposite qualities into a satisfying whole.

This chapter includes sample charts from Michael, Cynthia, and Jeff. After looking at the sample charts to see how it's done, you may wish to try creating your own charts. You'll find two blank worksheets, one each for Chart 1 and Chart 2, for you to use in mapping and evaluating your Tree of Life. You can simply put checkmarks under each quality, or if you prefer, you can go into greater detail, as did Michael, Cynthia, and Jeff. You can retrieve these details from the self-assessment lists you completed through the various exercises in earlier chapters.

Now, let's take a look at Michael, Cynthia, and Jeff's charts. From these, you can see simply and graphically how the faces of their personalities line up on their respective trees. Reviewing these sample charts might also help you see yourself more clearly and where your qualities would line up on your map.

Michael's Chart 1
How Michael's Tree of Life Looked in the Beginning

	Contracting	Balanced	Expanding
MIND	UNDERSTANDING	KNOWLEDGE	WISDOM (INTUITION)
	Over-editing self		
	Over-intellectualizing		
	Compulsive about details		
	Computer-like		
EMOTION	STRENGTH (DISCERNMENT)	COMPASSION	LOVE
	Overly critical of self and others		
	Projected "strong," appeared arrogant		
	Closed down		
ACTION	RECEPTIVITY	STABILITY	DOMINION (TAKING CHARGE)
	Stalled, unable to act		
	Difficulty receiving		
	Over-monitored family		

COMMENTS: Ex-military officer Michael's assessment of himself showed he was overly structured, contained, and blocked on the left side. He wanted to open the right side of Intuition and heart to express happiness, trust, give more love to others and himself, and go with the flow from an inspired place.

Michael's Chart 2
What Michael's Tree of Life Needed for Balance

	Contracting	*Balanced*	*Expanding*
MIND	UNDERSTANDING	KNOWLEDGE	WISDOM (INTUITION) Learn to trust intuition Go with the flow Loosen up to develop creativity Stop censoring self and others
EMOTION	STRENGTH (DISCERNMENT)	COMPASSION	LOVE Learn sensitivity Become more open Feel more hopitable and gentle
ACTIONS	RECEPTIVITY Receiving more Allowing things to emerge	STABILITY	DOMINION (TAKING CHARGE) Act assertively Exude confidence

COMMENTS: Michael needed to open up his right side of creativity and heart to find his true calling and to take positive action to make his career dreams come true. He needed to develop the right side of his tree and trim back his left side, bringing him closer to the middle trunk values of Compassion and Stability.

Cynthia's Chart 1
How Cynthia's Tree of Life Looked in the Beginning

	Contracting	*Balanced*	*Expanding*
MIND	UNDERSTANDING	KNOWLEDGE	WISDOM (INTUITION)
	Extremely intelligent		Intuitive, not
	Hid behind intellect,		trusting it
	discipline,		Unfocused, too much
	abstractions		imagination
EMOTION	STRENGTH (DISCERNMENT)	COMPASSION	LOVE
	Sometimes cool,		Over-giving
	withdrawn		Placating; unable to
			set boundaries,
			say no
			Self-sacrificing
ACTION	RECEPTIVITY	STABILITY	DOMINION (TAKING CHARGE)
	Acquiescent,		Overprotective
	non-assertive		Gave too much to
	Unable to receive		others
			Did not express needs

COMMENTS: Homemaker, mother, and teacher Cynthia was imbalanced on both the left and right sides of her tree. She vacillated between being overly giving and distancing herself when she wasn't getting what she needed. She knew she wanted to more directly assert her needs at work and home without feeling guilty or self-effacing. She wanted to broaden her horizons.

Cynthia's Chart 2
What Cynthia's Tree of Life Needed for Balance

	Contracting	Balanced	Expanding
MIND	UNDERSTANDING	KNOWLEDGE	WISDOM (INTUITION)
	Learn to be more direct and clear Better utilize deductive powers and logic		Trust her own instincts Go more with the flow Use intuition to make better decisions
EMOTION	STRENGTH (DISCERNMENT) Set clear boundaries Use better judgment Employ balanced independence Clarify wants and needs Say no or yes with conviction	COMPASSION	LOVE Love self more Treat others more lovingly
ACTION	RECEPTIVITY Receive better from others Accept recognition	STABILITY	DOMINION (TAKING CHARGE) Assert needs Achieve success in the world Take leadership positions

COMMENTS: Cynthia wanted to actualize herself. She needed to correct imbalances that had evolved from childhood restrictions. She wanted to develop the courage to liberate her talents and her spirit, enabling her to give more judiciously and to receive on a larger scale. She needed to learn to be direct and clear as well as to strengthen her kingdom, Dominion.

Jeff's Chart 1
How Jeff's Tree of Life Looked in the Beginning

	Contracting	Balanced	Expanding
MIND	UNDERSTANDING	KNOWLEDGE	WISDOM (INTUITION) Overplayed his hunches Sometimes acted irrationally Ungrounded
EMOTION	STRENGTH (DISCERNMENT)	COMPASSION	LOVE Over-generous, gave too much to others at work Held back, gave too little at home Credited others excessively, did not credit self enough
ACTION	RECEPTIVITY	STABILITY	DOMINION (TAKING CHARGE) Impulsive Overloaded at work, no time for self or family Overextended self, difficulty delegating Went in too many directions at once

COMMENTS: Entrepreneur Jeff is a dynamo! But he was scattered and anxious about being overextended and not controlling how fast he was expanding. He was extremely out of balance on the expansive right side of his tree. He felt panicky about his lack of controls. He wanted to give more to his family and less at work, so he could better enjoy his success and money.

Jeff's Chart 2
What Jeff's Tree of Life Needed for Balance

	Contracting	Balanced	Expanding
MIND	UNDERSTANDING Pay attention to details Think through issues Develop long-term strategies, goals	KNOWLEDGE	WISDOM (INTUITION)

EMOTION	STRENGTH
	(DISCERNMENT)
	Exercise greater disci-
	  pline at work
	Schedule time and
	  activities for self
	Use better judgment
	Establish boundaries and
	  limits to free up time
	  and money for self
		COMPASSION	LOVE
			
			Give more at home

ACTION	RECEPTIVITY
	Receive more for himself
	Take breaks, time to
	  smell the roses
	Take more vacations
	  with family
	Discern where and
	  when to expand
	Delegate more tasks
	Use better judgment in
	  spending money
		STABILITY	DOMINION
			(TAKING CHARGE)

COMMENTS: Jeff wants to be a dynamo with greater focus and control. He needs to delegate, expand intelligently, establish self-monitoring systems, and trust people to help him. He must learn not to overextend at work, so he can nurture himself and give more to his family. To give himself time and peace of mind to enjoy his successes, he needs a more balanced tree on a much firmer foundation.

Chart 1
How My Tree of Life Looks Now

Put a checkmark under each quality that is largely imbalanced in you at this time or list the ways in which you are out of balance in each quality. (See sample charts.) You can write any notes you wish under comments.

	Contracting	*Balanced*	*Expanding*
MIND	UNDERSTANDING	KNOWLEDGE	WISDOM (INTUITION)
EMOTION	STRENGTH (DISCERNMENT)	COMPASSION	LOVE
ACTION	RECEPTIVITY	STABILITY	DOMINION (TAKING CHARGE)

COMMENTS:
_____
_____
_____
_____
_____

CHART 2

What My Tree of Life Needs for Balance

Put a checkmark under each quality in which you need to cultivate balance or list your goals for that quality. You can write any
notes you wish under comments.

	Contracting	*Balanced*	*Expanding*
MIND	UNDERSTANDING	KNOWLEDGE	WISDOM (INTUITION)
EMOTION	STRENGTH (DISCERNMENT)	COMPASSION	LOVE
ACTION	RECEPTIVITY	STABILITY	DOMINION (TAKING CHARGE)

COMMENTS:

_____

_____

_____

_____

_____

Summaries of Michael, Cynthia and Jeff

Michael was glad to shed the mask of his former overly analytical self, the commanding officer who used to sternly give orders to military men. He connected to his ancestors and healed his childhood wounds, opened his heart, and envisioned fulfilling his long-hidden dream. He employed all his newfound skills in balancing himself, being more receptive to others, and opening himself to opportunities. This in turn activated his lower realm of Action and helped him find new creative work. He now enjoys gently teaching young children. His skills, his caring, and his open heart are warmly appreciated by the children and their parents. He revels in this realized dream, which nourishes his soul and allows him to give love to the world.

Cynthia is an inspiring example of an intelligent, but formerly self-effacing and nonassertive, woman who blossomed by utilizing her full potential. Once she realized she had been subjugating her needs to those of others, she changed! She became clearer about what she wanted to do. Upsetting the status quo and establishing her new foundation of stability took courage and determination. She peeled off the masks of insecurity and fear and allowed her faces to radiate, and as a result gained recognition as a highly respected, pioneering educator. As she embraced her Strength, her face of Love shone and brought more success at work and in her personal relationships.

Jeff changed himself from an over-the-top, out-of-control executive wearing a mask of anxiety into a balanced person who is successful in all aspects of his life. He not only did a better job of monitoring his company by balancing the budget, but he also expanded responsibly and created new, solid business opportunities. He learned to take better care of himself, which gave him the will and desire to delegate more tasks. He spent more time with his family. He created a very stable foundation and felt tremendously empowered with all his faces aglow with peace of mind and self-satisfaction. He now has time to enjoy his successes and to truly reign as the creator of his kingdom!

part seven

ultimate unity: becoming one with your many faces

Introduction

The ultimate goal of embracing the Tree of Life teachings is to align your thoughts, feelings and actions to reach your highest potential! Part seven is written to stimulate your creativity toward unifying all that you learned and put it into action in all facets of your life!

chapter fifteen

The End Is Embedded
in the Beginning—Unity

In a virgin forest, growth keeps pace with decay: at one place a tree will be reaching maturity, at another declining. As an old tree falls a gap is made in the canopy, light is let in and many younger trees reach with each other to occupy this new opening. This is happening by slow degrees throughout the forest and so the rhythm of growth is maintained.

—RICHARD ST. BARB BAKER, *MAN OF THE TREES*

Acquiring the Lost Knowledge

The goal of the Tree of Life journey is spiritual wholeness. This journey involves a revelatory pilgrimage back to your roots—whatever your culture, religion, or ethnicity—for the purpose of refining your character to bring you inner balance, peace, and joy. Tapping into the wisdom of your Tree of Life can transform fear, insecurity, and cynicism into open-hearted, open-minded, and courageous action. You then can simultaneously generate the quality that softens you as well as the quality that strengthens you. Your mind liberates, your emotions stabilize, and your body lightens. You live authentically, true to others and to yourself. You become hero and lover. You evolve into a perfectly symmetrical tree, nature's ultimate

work of art. Finally, you make an electrifying connection with the
Highest Power and radiate with the supreme gift of the Endless
Light: The Lost Knowledge.

The Tree of Life teachings guide us toward a "hidden" face in our
upper branches, representing full Knowledge (*Daat*). Your complete
face of Knowledge emerges from the shadows of your branches only
when your whole tree is balanced. As you have worked on your inner
tree and cultivated your branches and attributes, you no doubt have
experienced flashes of this upper Knowledge and the accompanying
ecstasy of total alignment. These moments of true enlightenment fill
you with a sense of wholeness and recharge your life force.

It is said the new millennium is the age of complete harmony, a
time for aligning the realms of mind, emotion, and action. The great
Western religions believe this is the Messianic Age. The Christian
faith hails it as the season of the second coming of Christ. The Jewish
faith considers it to be the time of the first coming of the Messiah.

*The ancient Kabbalah reveals that the Messiah represents a state of
human consciousness in which we all become the empowered leaders
of our respective lives by reconnecting with our ancestral roots and the
Higher Power.*

These empowered people consequently take greater responsibility
for their individual lives as well as in the world at large. Their mission
is to do their utmost to make the whole earth a harmonious place. In
this era of inspired action, there will be many "King Davids" aligning
all their faces to restore balance to the kingdom of humanity. Each will
become loving warriors in his or her domain, joyfully assuming
responsibility for creating the lives they envision, building upon the
foundation of their inner truths and full Knowledge.

Completion means having intimate knowledge of all our qualities—mastering each of our faces individually, then uniting them
within a balanced center. When all our faces of spiritual light fuse
together, the results can be amazing! Our capacity to affect positive
change within and in the world becomes limitless. We can do anything
we set our minds to, make any dream come true, using the very laws of
nature to manifest that which we envision. Such are the rewards of
attaining Wisdom, and with it, the uppermost crown of Unity.

In the seed is contained the whole tree. When you balance all your branches of qualities and integrate all 10 faces of your soul, your glowing crown of Unity lights up your whole tree. You can experience simultaneously the vastness of the heavens, using your inherent creativity, and the vastness of your intertwined roots, using the stabilizing wisdom of your ancestors. This engenders the motivation to put these divine ideas into grounded action.

Inspired Actions: Unifying Your Life

This section will give you practical ideas to begin to integrate your insights into yourself regarding your need for balance. When you experience congruence between your thoughts and feelings, you'll want to take action in all areas of your life so that you can become one with daily actions at home, work, and in the greater community.

Building Global Foundations from Inner Stability

As we achieve greater balance and increased higher Wisdom, we discover new sources of inspiration and opportunities for positive action in the world. We receive intuitive flashes with increased frequency and act on them with higher efficiency and greater responsibility, all the while maintaining a serene inner balance. This spiritually driven, balanced momentum prepares us for life in the twenty-first century. On a very practical level, this acquired state of learned grace translates into mastery on the physical plane of existence.

You achieve this inner stability by recognizing your needs, respecting your limits, and cooperating with life's natural cycles. Because you are better able to give and receive, you operate with greater confidence in your relationships as well as within your local and global communities. Thinking, feeling, and functioning in a healthier way improves your physical health. It also enables you to improve the physical well-being of others and the environment.

With your roots grounded in ancestral Wisdom and your crown open to higher Knowledge, you shed antiquated patterns of restrictive thinking and destructive action (or reaction). You kick off tired attitudes about gender, class, and race that no longer fit—just like a worn-out pair of shoes. You place trust in yourself, others, nature, and the Creator, assured the universe *will* provide, if only we ask, help, and let it. You also recognize you are not the only tree in the forest and cannot control everything—and you no longer wish to. Instead, you release control to the heavens, extend all your branches, and connect with the vast woodland surrounding you. You receive and activate inspired ideas for creating the world you envision. No longer afraid of encroaching upon or being squeezed out by the other creatures of the forest, you live in harmony as an integral and productive member of your chosen kingdom on Earth.

Seeking Out Opposite Branches for Balance

Most of us instinctively gravitate toward people, places, and experiences that appeal to the imbalanced or more prominent qualities, which limit us and can throw us even further off-kilter. The Tree of Life process impels you to stretch your limbs! You experience an innate hunger to create a rich environment that embodies all the varying qualities on the different branches of the Tree of Life. In fact, as you work to balance these qualities within yourself, you are likely to bring into your life people who possess the faces of your soul you wish to develop. For example, a left-focused engineer may seek out a right-leaning sculptor and vice versa. An intellectual might join a gym to work on her body, perhaps for the first time, and make a love connection with the athletic trainer of her dreams. A heavy equipment operator may find himself suddenly engaged in lively conversation with a lawyer who frequents the same diner. Go-getters and sedentary folks reach out to each other for calm and stimulation, respectively. Youngsters seek the counsel of elders, while middle-agers seek the invigorating company of youth. Artisans who once eschewed monetary rewards in their blind pursuit of artistic gratification image into their lives generous patrons and more lucrative avenues to economic and creative balance. Those who have mastered the art of the deal turn to organic farming, trading in corporate stocks, and stress, for a backhoe and countryside strolls.

Sharing Roots

In America's intensely individualistic culture, people often feel isolated and out of place within their communities. Immigrants to the United States often jump head-first and hope-filled onto the "American dream" bandwagon, which frequently turns into a fast train to Lonelytown on the shores of Lake Disenchantment. Even those who "make it" often feel as alone as their native-born neighbors—a natural reaction to a fragmented society that physically and spiritually distances us from our "familiars."

Sometimes, it takes a village to complete a soul. Many of us become more acutely aware of this as we progress through our Tree of Life work. We can balance our qualities with those of the other members of our village—whether they come from our jobs, churches, synagogues, neighborhoods, clubs, genetic, or assembled families. We can reach out to and learn from immigrants from countries that place a greater emphasis on family and community. Many urban and suburban Americans are returning to less populated and rural areas in search of community. Others form villages marked with boundaries of spirit, rather than geography, bringing together people who share a specific commonality. Ethnic, artistic, and gay groups, especially, often create these unique villages. Still other people rally and ally their neighbors, creating surprisingly close-knit communities by today's standards, reminiscent of days gone by. The grassroots community preparedness programs that formed in response to the Y2K computer glitch and recent natural disasters are good examples of this.

You can consciously grow a forest that will help nurture your Tree of Life by first envisioning the kind of community you want. Who are your fellow villagers? What common goals and interests do they share? How do they, individually and collectively, utilize their qualities for the greater good of the community? Once you've envisioned your unique twenty-first-century village, you must network to fill it with balanced villagers who can give and receive in equal measure. You might extend your roots to an existing village or plant seeds and act as the master gardener to sprout a new one. When networking and interacting with other villagers, remember to use both discrimination and receptivity.

Business Blooms

As you gain mastery of the Tree of Life teachings, your enhanced intuitive and analytic abilities will help you make sound career and financial decisions. You'll know when to expand, acting on your visions, and when to contract, pruning your branches and cutting your losses.

What is more, opportunities will come to you. With your branches of Receptivity and Dominion in balance, business connections materialize. And money does grow on trees! Those who will thrive in the twenty-first century will be those who embrace their responsibility to serve humanity. They embody the adage "Doing well by doing good." They innovate new and improved ways to blend generosity with discernment, to combine capitalism with charity, and to produce good products and services along with genuine good will. Enlightened employers and employees of the third millennium balance Strength with Love, Dominion with Receptivity, and village with self. They share opportunities, rewards, and responsibilities equitably, without regard to gender, ethnicity, social, status, or any other falsely restrictive characteristic. They afford equal respect to Mr. Moms and Ms. Presidents, to homemakers, cab drivers, CEOs, scientists, teachers, and, yes, even writers. In this new age of harmony between material and spiritual advancement, the key operatives are flexibility, cooperation, trust, and greater freedom.

Stability in the Center of Chaos

The hallmark of living with all 10 faces of your soul in balance is the ability to remain centered no matter what imbalance or chaos swirls around you. When you achieve Stability in your trunk, you can weather the worst storms, knowing the valuable lessons you gain during the humbling descent is a normal part of your eventual ascent process. You learn to balance the polarities, the opposing forces, both within you and around you. You accept responsibility for your life and relish your self-sufficiency, knowing when to seek and accept help from others. You also know when to nurture your inner family and when to yield to the other members of your village. You stand tall, the co-creator of your Tree of Life, swaying gently in the winds of change, allowing nothing and no others to bend or break your boughs, or to uproot your foundation.

Maintaining Your Garden

As you stroll along in the harmonious garden of your life, having successfully cultivated all your branches, you will periodically need to do some maintenance on your tree and garden. Patches of weeds may pop up from the remnants of deeply imbedded roots you did not completely extricate previously or from new seeds of imbalance propagated within yourself or blown in from other people's gardens. But now, with your Tree of Life mastery, you can quickly discern invasive weeds from healthy new growth—and pluck them!

You also will occasionally need to prune back a branch that has slightly extended its reach and upset the symmetry of your tree. An uneasy "gut" feeling, headache, or stomachache may signal the time has come to get out your pruning shears. Perhaps you feel parched, which may indicate your tree thirsts for something new. Now, with your refined powers of divination, you'll know where to find and how to tap the healing waters to quench your thirst. Because you're in tune with your natural growth cycles, you quickly detect when your branches grow less vigorously, your foliage lacks luster, or your trunk weakens. Then you take action to provide your tree with the additional rest, protection from the elements, or nutrients it needs.

How do you tell when you're off balance? You always know. Your body tells you: with a headache (your upper branches), stomach ache (lower branches), or heartache (middle branches). Symptoms of imbalance manifest differently with each person. You must learn your body's distress signals and their unique meaning to you. From my personal experience and the experiences of my clients, I have gleaned some generalizations regarding how the body signals spiritual imbalance that seem to apply in many cases.

Headaches may mean you are spending too much time thinking about something that troubles or hurts you but not doing anything about it. Your Tree of Life work, however, has prepared you to stop obsessing, focus on the problem, and take action to resolve it. It could be something as simple as preparing a speech or a lesson plan or as major as changing careers or starting/ending a partnership. As you've learned through your earlier Tree of Life work, you might need to first let go—step back and allow your thoughts and feelings to emerge and align—and then trust yourself to just do it.

Heartache (literal, not angina) may mean you have slipped back into either loving too much or too little—either yourself or others.

The tree can help you determine when to say yes and when to say no, when to assert yourself and when to withdraw.

A bellyache signals the need for direct action, often a change in direction. Perhaps you're caught in a paralyzing cycle of zealously generating things to do—but not slowing down enough to get off the spinning wheel and get them done. Maybe you've been compulsively shopping, working, partying, or pursuing a love interest. Perhaps you temporarily switched off your self-monitor and overindulged in something that gave you enormous pleasure one moment, then it turned around the next and bit you. When you get stuck on any of your branches—in your thinking, emotions, or actions—you must put on the brakes. Only then can you discern which way to reach your goal: balance.

Exercise 31: Realigning Your Tree of Life

You can learn to align yourself (your inner tree) by paying attention to your head, heart, and belly. This requires paying particular attention to any subtle inner or outer reaction that may be revealing itself as pain or physical sensations.

Use the following meditation to regain your equilibrium.

1. Acknowledge you feel discomfort.
2. Focus on the area where you feel the distress.
3. Breathe in a slow, even, and relaxed way.
4. Visualize your whole Tree of Life emanating its life energy into the affected area.
5. Experience the thoughts, feelings, and images that tumble into your mind and body.
6. Verbally express your needs to yourself and others.
7. Envision the manifestation of your needs being met; see each affected branch healed and your whole tree in balance.
8. Take appropriate action to restore your balance.

Wholeness

As you come to the end of this book, we return to the important teaching of the Kabbalists introduced in chapter 1: The end is embedded in the beginning. The *Sefer Yetizrah* (*Book of Creation*) tells how a flame cannot exist without the coal. The coal is the middleman, both the receptacle and the distributor of the flame. It spontaneously takes in, holds, and then gives out the major properties of the flame: light and warmth. Just as the coal absorbs the flame to then discharge its energy, so, too, must we receive the Eternal Light to then traject its life force into the world. The Tree of Life teachings inform us and prepare us to both openly receive and graciously give back. When we balance ourselves, we instinctively meditate on how we can use the stable trunks, fully cultivated branches, and expansive root systems of our individual trees to help the entire forest evolve.

All the branches of the Tree of Life receive sustenance from its roots and from the sun (Endless Light). The roots circulate nutrients up through the trunk to all the branches (faces) and foliage, while the sun beams spiritual energy into the tree from above.

As you probably have discovered, the 10 faces of your soul are intertwined. Just as the end is embedded in the beginning, each of your faces contains all the other faces. Your glowing face of Unity is coalescence of the individual faces of Unity, Wisdom, Understanding, Love, Strength, Compassion, Dominion, Receptivity, Stability, and Faith. The face of Understanding fuses not only with the face of Wisdom, but also with the faces of Love and Strength, and so on, blending all 10 faces of the soul in all possible combinations. The secret of the Tree of Life is that each of your faces reflect the whole of the original fragmented sparks of life that came from the Endless Light. Through uniting our many faces, we learn to absorb and synthesize this Light and to project out the inner glow we rediscover. As we achieve greater balance and act responsibly from a stable foundation and the inspiration of a Higher Power, opportunities emerge. We receive visions of ways in which we can contribute to the betterment of ourselves, our lives, others, and the world. These inspired acts of goodness come not from a sense of "should" or "must," but from the genuine need and desire to branch out from the joy and strength we derive from actualizing our potentials.

Now that you've reached the end of this journey—cultivating your Tree of Life through completing this book—a new journey begins. You've peeled back the outer husks protecting your 10 faces—releasing their hidden light and restoring your spiritual nature and authentic self. You are ready to continue the act of creation, to go forth and propagate spiritual balance in the world. The end is embedded in the beginning. All is contained within the seed. Now plant your seeds of a new genesis.

I'd like to leave you with a final meditation to help you forge ahead in the new millennium on your journey toward wholeness. Once you achieve greater balance on your Tree of Life, you will be inspired to pursue new dreams, new roles, new careers, new activities. You can become whatever you want to be, manifest whatever you want in your life, reflecting your unique essence.

Exercise 32: New Millennium Meditation

1. Close your eyes. Focus on your breathing, inhaling and exhaling deeply and evenly. Gently feel the life force of the air moving in and out. Take a deep breath quickly through your nose, hold it, let it out slowly through your mouth. Repeat this sharp breathing two more times. As you take these deep breaths, envision yourself as a whole tree with symmetrical branches, an upright trunk, and an expansive network of roots firmly planted in the ground. Your tree is healthy and full of vitality. The upper branches reach up into the heavens, conjoining with your Higher Power.

(Continued on next page)

(Continued from previous page)

2. Take refuge in the comfort of your balanced Tree of Life. Feel the power of its invigorating, yet nurturing, energy coursing through your stable trunk and steady branches. Experience and express your gratitude toward the life force that sustains you and enables you to thrive.

3. See yourself capturing new seeds created by your healthy tree. Image growing in new directions, expanding to a different grove, or perhaps transplanting to a different forest altogether. Perhaps you image yourself in a new relationship or career. Exploring a new interest or activity. Relating differently with your children, spouse, coworkers, or friends. Tackling a difficult project you've avoided but now feel inspired to pursue. Envision your simplest and grandest dreams.

4. Visualize planting these new seeds in fertile soil in the environment that will nurture them. Visualize yourself in your new dominion, supported by your ancestral roots of reverence and graced with the blessing of your higher spirit. Your spirit surges up your stable trunk and through your lush branches. United in spirit, the energy fields of your balanced branches hum together in perfect harmony, lighting up your whole tree and unmasking the 10 glowing faces of your soul.

The Tree of Life Operating
in the Creation of this Book

Sheldon and I don't claim to have balanced our whole trees yet. We're both still in the process. While collaborating on this book, we have learned much about our Trees of Life and experienced both challenging and exhilarating moments in working with our various faces. We successfully used some of the Tree of Life techniques to smooth out the inevitable rough patches along the way. We also had fun—a very good indication, to me, that applying the Tree of Life concepts can bring joy to our lives.

When my phone rang one warm May night in Flowery Branch, Georgia, in 1996, I had no premonition that an exotic, uncharted world was about to open to me. However, I was receptive (*Hod*) to the caller, Dr. Sheldon Z. Kramer of San Diego, California, because my friend Hal Zina Bennett had referred him to me. Although his proposal to help him with his book intrigued me, I found myself monitoring with my left branch of Strength (*Gevurah*), balancing the offer of work with my desire to take action (*Dominion*) on my own books.

As I listened to him relate his story, however, I sensed his love (*Chesed*) and passion for his work. When he explained some of the concepts of his ideas and teachings, I immediately understood (*Binah*) the importance and ramifications of giving the gift

(*Netzach*) of this book to the world. The electrifying light of divine inspiration (*Chokmah*) virtually sparked through the telephone wires as I intuitively realized (*Binah*) this work would engage my heart! During that conversation, I think we both relished the recognition of another expansive soul and intuited we would work well together.

From that inspired moment on, we began the work of balancing our exuberant natures (right side of the tree) with discernment (left side of the tree). At one point Sheldon felt he had been too expansive (right side) in putting so much time and money on this book. So, he pulled back and put it in the drawer (Receptivity) for a while to devote more time to his clients and to earning money rather than spending it.

I credit this very fine psychologist, spiritual coach, and friend with getting the collaboration off to a wonderful start and facilitating an equal partnership from the beginning. He sensed my former distrust of men and showed compassion (*Tiferet*), rather than defensiveness, which fostered my faith (*Malchut*) in him and in our ability to forge a partnership. He was always receptive (*Hod*) to what I needed to make it work. I was proud of myself for speaking up with Strength (*Gevurah*) and honesty to say that, if I were to do his book, I would need his support to work on my book at the same time. In the past, I would have thrown myself off balance by overextending my right side to please (*Chesed*), overgiving at my expense, or by thinking a man's project was more important than mine.

Sheldon agreed to these dual objectives. In fact, he coached me to send him pages of my book, just as I coached him to send me pages of this book. With the kind support (*Chesed*) and feedback of Sheldon's generous wife, Carmela, we took action (*Netzach*) to create both books and a movie treatment as well! His generous strategy worked for him, because we finished this book and got a publishing contract for it first. It worked for me as well, because I gained the honor of having my name on this valuable book and made progress on my book. What is more, the project with Sheldon led to additional book collaborations with others: job security with increasing financial stability (*Yesod*). So you see, this Tree of Life stuff really works!

We also experienced great joy from the process of creating the book. Flashes of inspiration would come to us from above, and we'd ride the high, creating with broad strokes and rich colors. Then we'd ground ourselves to carefully add the details. Sometimes, we'd sway too far left and right, getting carried away with right-brain over-expansiveness (overwriting) and then bogging down in left-brain obsessiveness over minutia. We wrestled with one another and with our compassionate, savvy editor at Adams, Paula Munier Lee, to reach the fine balance of providing substantive and accessible information on a complex, somewhat ethereal, subject matter. Of course, only you, the reader, can tell us whether we have succeeded. Since Kabbalah focuses on balancing opposing energies, Sheldon was glad to integrate a feminine perspective with his masculine point of view, although we sometimes switched places in that regard as well.

We didn't consciously plan a certain number of chapters or parts in the book. As we went through many drafts and many ways to organize this book, its structure continually changed. Mysteriously, the book evolved, as if of its own volition, into its present form of seven major parts. Shortly after, while writing about the number seven's importance in Tree of Life wisdom (the seven faces relating to the seven days of the Creation), we suddenly looked at one another in shared recognition. We wouldn't be at all surprised if there were some hidden significance here!

Sheldon and I would occasionally engage in heated conversations over differences of opinion, particularly concerning negotiations with agents and publishers. "I know you, Mardeene, and you're too heavily weighted on the right side of your tree!" Sheldon would say. "You really need to be stronger, and we need to be more discerning!" To which I would retort, "Sheldon, where's the faith you wrote about under the section on *Malchut*? Why do you worry?" Then we'd both laugh and work our way back to a more productive collaborative balance, taking pleasure in knowing one another that well and having fun with the tree.

By applying our Tree of Life lessons to our collaboration, we managed to stay balanced throughout the process, individually and in our partnership, even during conflicts, which is rare. We trusted one another and had faith we could work out anything for our mutual benefits and for the ultimate benefit of the book.

We invite you to engage in this very satisfying process with your self-development, your relationships with loved ones, and your work. I guarantee you will be richly rewarded for your efforts. We'd love to hear about your Tree of Life experiences.

—MARDEENE BURR MITCHELL

For more information about the Tree of Life teachings, or to contact Dr. Kramer:

Sheldon Z. Kramer, Ph.D.
P.O. Box 927828
San Diego, California 92192-7828
E-Mail: SkramerPhd@aol.com

To contact Mardeene Burr Mitchell:
E-mail: Mardeene@mindspring.com

Assagioli, R. *The Act of Will*. Penguin, 1973.

_____. *Psychosynthesis*. Viking Press, 1965.

Baker, Richard St. Barbe. *Man of the Trees*. Willits, Calif: Ecology Action, 1989.

Breslov, Rabbi Nathan. *Rabbi Nachman: Advice*. Translated from the Hebrew by A. Greenbaum. New York: Breslov Research Institute, 1983.

Holy Bible, Old and New Testaments, Revised Standard Version. New York: Thomas Nelson and Sons.

Horan, Martin. *The Little Book of Jewish Wisdom*. Rockport, Mass: Element Books, Ltd., 1995.

Idel, Moishe. *Kabbalah: New Perspectives*. Yale University Press, 1998.

Kaplan, Aryeh. *Chasidic Masters*. Brooklyn, New York: Monznaim Publisher, 1984.

_____. *Inner Space*. Brooklyn, New York: Monznaim Publisher, 1990.

_____. *Meditation and the Bible*. York Beach, Maine: Samuel Weiser, 1978.

_____. *Meditation in Kabbalah*. York Beach, Maine: Samuel Weiser, 1982.

_____. *Sefer Yetzirah: The Book of Creation*. York Beach, Maine: Samuel Weiser, 1990.

Kramer, Dr. Sheldon Z. Jewish Meditation: Healing Ourselves and Our Relationships. Chap. 13 in *Opening the Inner Gates, New Paths in Kabbalah and Psychology*, edited by Edward Hoffman. New York: Four Worlds Press, 1995.

_____. *Transforming the Inner and Outer Family: Humanistic and Spiritual Approaches to Mind–Body Systems Therapy*. New York: Haworth Press, 1995.

Krauss, Ruth. *The Carrot Seed*. New York: Harper and Row, 1945.

"The Tree of Life." In the *Magazine Parobola: Myth and Tradition*. Fall, 1989.

Polsky, H. W. and Wozner, Waella. *Everyday Miracles: The Healing Wisdom of Hasidic Stories*. New York: Jason Aronson, 1989.

Weinstein, Avi. *Gates of Light* San Francisco: HarperCollins.

index

Authors' Biographies

Sheldon Z. Kramer, Ph.D. is a licensed clinical psychologist in full-time private practice in San Diego, California. He holds degrees in both psychology and comparative religion and his specialty is integrating ancient wisdom—mind-body medicine with modern psychological principles. He speaks and coaches CEOs, entertainment industry, and health care professionals internationally. To contact Dr. Kramer: Sheldon Z. Kramer, Ph.D., P.O. Box 927828, San Diego, CA 92192-7828, or by e-mail: SkramerPhd@aol.com.

Mardeene Burr Mitchell, former executive director of Writers Connection in Silicon Valley, California, is a freelance writer/photographer/editor, writing coach, and speaker. She has collaborated on numerous book and screenplay projects. She is marketing her own photostory book and television series based upon the book. One of her screenplays was a finalist in The Best in the West Screenplay Competition and has been optioned by a producer. She is on the Board of Directors of Women in Film/Atlanta, Georgia and is in progress on her second book. To contact Mardeene Burr Mitchell: E-mail: Mardeene@mindspring.com